Purnell's Animals of the World
Europe

Purnell's Animals of the World
Europe

Maria Pia and **Alessandro Minelli**

Designed by **Gabriele Pozzi**
Translated by **Bruce Penman**
Edited by **Brenda Ralph Lewis**

Purnell

PREFACE

The Animals of the World is a series in nine volumes which carries us on a fascinating journey through the varied and colourful animal kingdom and its countless natural environments.

In each continent we shall take a good look at some of the most typical members of the major groups of animals, and through the pages of these nine volumes, lavishly illustrated with both photographs and drawings, we shall see how life is lived in forest and clearing, on the wide prairie or inaccessible mountain-top, in a swift, clear stream or slow-moving jungle river, amid polar ice or burning desert sands. Everywhere animal life is confronted with the eternal problem of survival, the search for shelter from the pitiless rays of the sun, for a means of escape from hungry and cunning predators, for adequate supplies of food in time of shortage, or for a place to build a nest, lay eggs and reproduce.

Every living animal has found its own answers to these problems. Some have learned to hide from their enemies, and some to challenge them in defence of their own right to live. The periophthalmus, a small fish living in the coastal waters of Asia, often leaves the water and runs about on the mud. The dipper is a land bird that has learned to use its wings to fly under water. There are the poisonous coral snakes, whose brilliant colouring serves as a warning to would-be aggressors to keep their distance; and then there are other, similarly coloured, non-poisonous snakes which are protected solely by their resemblance to the poisonous coral snakes.

In fact, strategies for survival are almost as numerous as the species that practise them. And the nine volumes of this series describe the most important of these varied answers to the basic problem of survival in so many different environments.

ISBN 0 361 06596 5
Copyright © 1983 Arnoldo Mondadori Editore S.p.A., Milan
English translation copyright © 1984
Arnoldo Mondadori Editore S.p.A., Milan
Published 1984 by Purnell Books,
Paulton, Bristol BS18 5LQ, a member of the BPCC Group
Printed and bound in Spain
by Artes Graficas Toledo S.A.
D. L. TO: 1188 -1984

CONTENTS

Marmots in the Alps

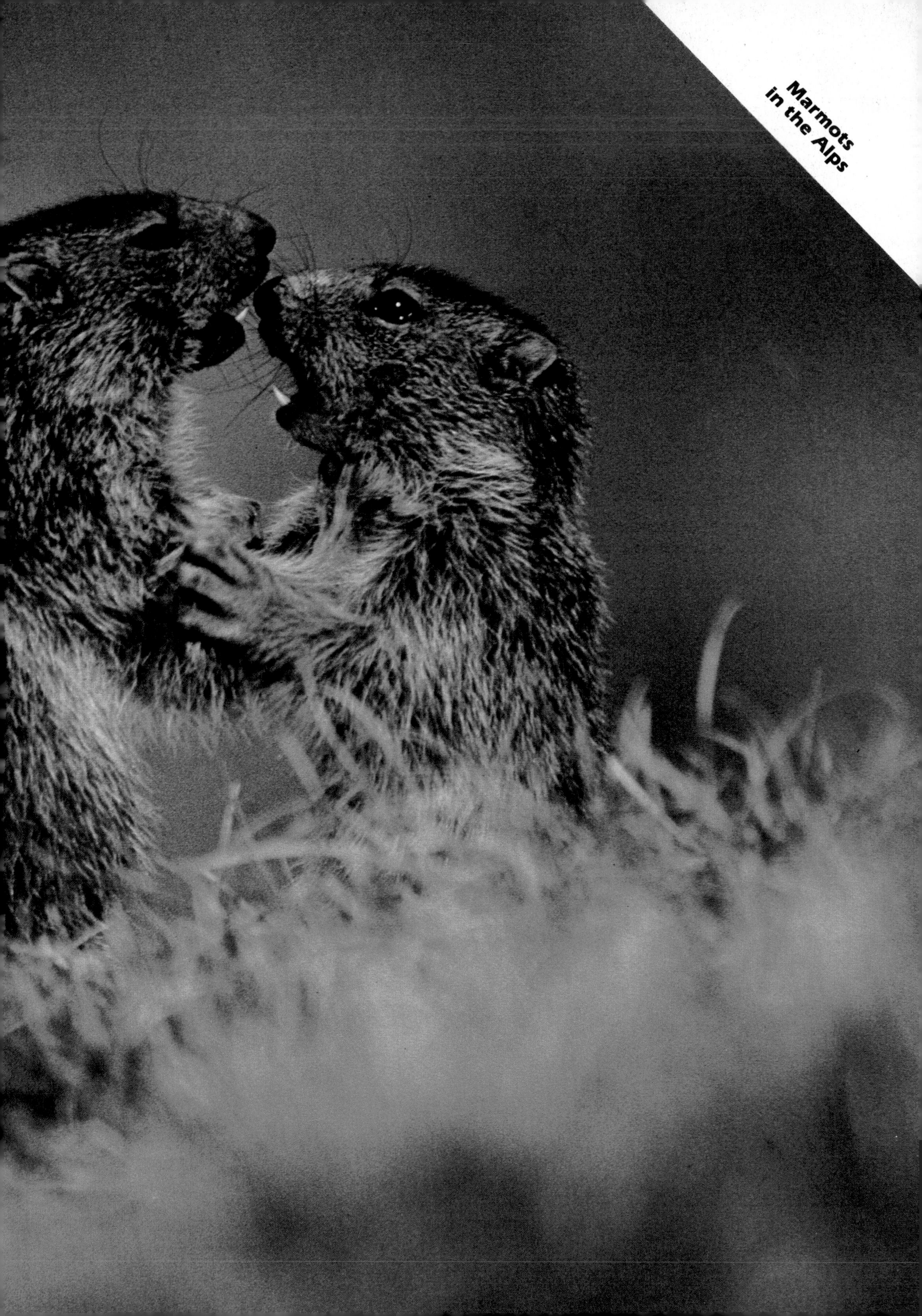

EUROPE: A BIRD'S EYE VIEW

Europe is the world's second smallest continent, but it is very heavily populated and has a huge network of roads. Once, long ago, Europe was covered in thick forests where deer, wolves, hares and other animals made their homes. Now, many forests have been cut down and rich crop-fields have taken their place. Even so, in many parts of Europe forest and grasslands still remain. Here you can still see the bright colours of nature in the countryside, as well as rivers, lakes and swamps. In some places, like northern France, there are sand dunes. The Alps mountains have snow-covered peaks and rocky slopes dotted with tiny flowers. Even in the towns and cities, broad avenues are lined with trees and people grow flowers, bushes, fruit trees and vegetables in their gardens. In summer, these gardens are full of birds, butterflies and insects. Even wild animals, like foxes, may live in the towns.

However, many animals could not survive in towns, among them creatures which have been hunted for their fur, skins or horns—like ibex or chamois. With the eagle, which has been hunted for its feathers, ibex and chamois now live high in the Alps where it is hard for the hunters to reach them.

Many other creatures also live among the shady woods of beech, pine, fir and oak in the Alps. Many live on the sunny mountainsides. There are woodpeckers, hard at work digging out insects from the bark of old trees. Squirrels leap from branch to branch looking for food: they like hazelnuts, and crack them to get out the kernels, the tasty nut-centres. Squirrels also like pine-seeds and strip off the outsides of pine-cones to reach them. In grassy clearings among the thick woods, you can find stags and big brown bears.

Beyond the woodlands, meadows and pastures look like wide carpets of short grass laid on the ground. Where there is plenty of water, the grass is rich green and grows thickly. Multicoloured butterflies live here, and brilliant flowers grow. Beneath the grass live moles, vole-rats, earthworms and mole-crickets. Great swarms of ants raid the meadows for food. Overhead, hawks fly high in the sky. At night, the countryside is peaceful. Only the crickets cry or the owls hoot sadly. Flitting fireflies make tiny spots of light in the dark, which is their way of sending messages.

Mountain streams flow swiftly between the rocks, then foam through mountain ravines, then slow down on reaching the wider part of the valley. The stream may plunge into lake and flow through it. It comes out of the far end of the lake as a muddy river, moving slowly towards the sea. The otters who live on the banks and get their food from the river are marvellous swimmers. They dive into the water, catch fish and swim back to the bank holding the fish in their mouths.

In the marshes, where reeds grow thickly in shallow water,

Europe has a wider range of landscapes than most other parts of the world. This is why there are great differences in Europe's climates and why a rich range of fauna or animals can live there. As the map shows, some animals live in the icy north near the Arctic Circle. Others prefer the sunny shores of the Mediterranean.

1. otter
2. salmon
3. roe deer
4. polecat
5. marmot
6. fallow deer
7. Egyptian vulture
8. jay
9. dormouse
10. beaver
11. flamingo
12. kingfisher
13. eagle
14. mole
15. grey heron
16. ibex
17. hedgehog
18. viper
19. wild boar
20. porcupine
21. squirrel
22. weasel
23. griffon vulture
24. green woodpecker
25. wolf
26. pine-marten
27. red deer
28. capercailzie
29. stork
30. badger
31. shrew
32. wild cat
33. eagle owl
34. eel
35. water-vole
36. brown bear
37. lynx
38. cuckoo
39. fox

frogs and tadpoles live. Dragonflies swiftly dart about. Ducks rest in the marshes during their long migrations, when they fly from one home to another. On dunes near the sea, the sand is warmed by the summer sun and is full of insects. Nearby, the loud cries of insects called cicadas sound from the scrubland that lies beyond the beach.

Though small, Europe is very old and very varied. In the far north, in Norway or northern Russia, it is very cold. In the south, in Italy, Spain, Greece and around the Mediterranean Sea, it is hot and sunny. This book takes you on a thrilling journey across this fascinating continent—from the high Alps mountains, through woods, meadows, pastures, springs, rivers, lakes, to sand dunes and scrubland close to the sea. Everywhere, there is animal life.

1

2

This is how the snow-covered peaks of the Alps look to a bird flying high above. The mountain tops are clearly outlined in the sunshine (3). Mountains are one of the many "faces" of Europe. Europe also has rivers which flow swiftly in their upper reaches, but slow down as they get near to the sea (1). Another "face" of Europe can be seen in the dense scrub that lines the Mediterranean coast: this scrub is full of light and shade (2). A great part of Europe is covered by flowery meadows and pastures (4). This is a wonderful place for butterflies and millions of other insects. There are also great woods of pine, fir and beech trees (5). Here, you can find the red deer with its beautiful antlers, the brown bear, and the shy, graceful roebuck.

3 4

5

THE ALPS

Climbing up a high mountain is rather like travelling northwards, for the higher you go, the colder it gets. As you climb, the scenery changes. You start among shady woods of oak and beech. Further up, there are fir and larch trees. Then you find low thickets of myrtle and twisted dwarf birch trees. Finally, you reach the region of snow and ice, where the soil is stony: here, leaves and flowers can grow only during the very short summer. All the way up, though, there is animal, bird and insect life. There is life in the sunny pastures and woodlands, the rocky heights where the ibex lives and also in the sky, where the eagle looks down on the mountains from above.

1. wall-creeper
2. weasel
3. common lizard
4. alpine rosalia beetle
5. blackcock
6. millepede
7. reticulate carabid beetle
8. golden carabid beetle
9. centipede
10. tiger-beetle
11. eagle owl
12. lynx
13. ermine
14. snow-vole
15. snail
16. buzzard
17. hazel grouse
18. wild cat
19. wolf
20. capercailzie
21. alpine hare
22. salamander
23. alpine shrew
24. dipper
25. alpine chough
26. eagle
27. ibex
28. chamois
29. alpine swift
30. ptarmigan
31. common chough
32. *Parnassus* butterfly
33. tiger-moth
34. marmot
35. argus butterfly
36. *Endrosa* butterfly

Life among the rocks

It is soon after dawn. The sun cannot be seen yet above the snow-covered mountains, but the sky is clear and full of light. The wind, blowing up from the valley, stirs the bushes and grass growing on the heights above. A stream rushes downwards among the rocks. Somewhere round here are the chamois. They can be difficult to find, even if you follow their tracks for days. You may know the places where they rest, and the rough pastures where they feed: you may also know the rocky mountain crags and steep valleys which they climb so boldly on their little hoofs. But the chamois are very shy and nervous. If they smell people nearby, they usually run away. If you are lucky, though, you will see a herd of chamois, perhaps on a rocky slope where there are still traces of snow in crevices sheltered from the sun. The herd consists of about ten chamois. Some are mothers, accompanied by their newborn kids; some are yearling females, only a few months old and so still too young to have their own kids. The adult males are nowhere to be seen. They are proud and solitary creatures, and are hidden somewhere among the rocks.

2

1

It is very difficult to survive in the harsh conditions of the high mountains. Not many animals can live here. But the ibex (1) and the chamois (2, 3) can do so, and both make their home on the steep mountain crags. Somehow these animals manage to find enough to eat among the stunted vegetation between the snow-covered boulders on the very highest mountain pastures.

3

Life is not easy for creatures who live high in the mountains. Here, the soil is covered with snow and ice for month after month. Winter ends suddenly and quickly, but the season of sunshine and flowers that follows is very short. It is too short to banish the frost, which soon returns to the mountain in full force. The southern slopes, where the sun shines more often and the winter is shorter, is the home of the ibex, the wild goat of the Alps. The male ibex is a fierce-looking animal, over a metre long, with strong, curved horns.

These horns can be very dangerous. When two ibexes fight,

22

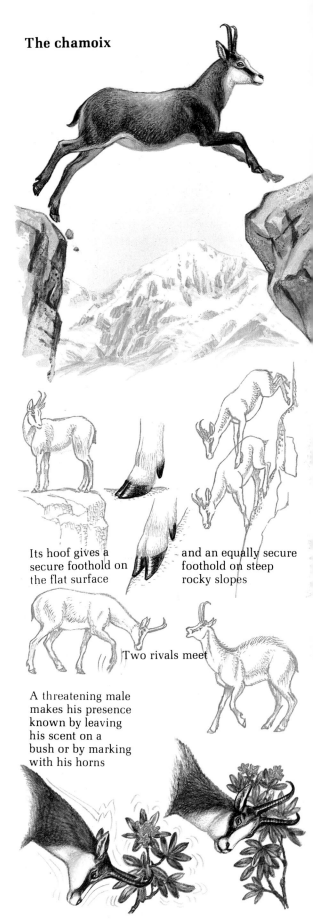

The chamoix

Its hoof gives a secure foothold on the flat surface

and an equally secure foothold on steep rocky slopes

Two rivals meet

A threatening male makes his presence known by leaving his scent on a bush or by marking with his horns

each lowers its head so that its horns stick out, like curved swords. It rushes towards it opponent, and it seems certain the two contestants will be badly injured or even killed. Fortunately, these fights are not very serious. Ibexes can butt each other with their horns for quite a long time, but no blood is shed. The fight is really a test of strength, determination and endurance. Its purpose is to see which ibex is the best one to be leader of the herd.

Newly-born male ibexes are happy to stay with their mothers as part of the herd but later, when they are older, they will wander off on their own. Then, they will start quarrelling and fighting among themselves. Very old male ibexes are much calmer, though. If an ibex reaches the ripe old age of twelve or more, he will not be so interested in fighting. These old ibexes look very dignified and majestic with their long horns, and they prefer to live a quieter life alone among the mountains.

The golden eagle

Eagles' nests lie among rocks, far away from the mountain paths people use. Sometimes, eagles nest on a remote cliff-face only birds can reach. They spend all day soaring and wheeling about the sky, searching for food. They have wonderful eyesight and can see a tiny marmot sitting on guard by its burrow, or a crow flying 1,000 metres (over 3,000 ft) below. Silently, swiftly, the eagle swoops down on its prey and seizes it in its curved claws. Death comes quickly, for the prey has no time to fight the eagle or get away. If the eagle wants a meal for itself, its sharp hooked beak at once tears into its prey and the unfortunate creature is eaten in five minutes, or less. However, the eagle may have a family of eaglets waiting for food in the nest. If so, then the prey is carried home in one piece and is torn apart in the nest for the eaglets to share. Young eagles grow up quickly. When they are only three months old, they are ready to leave the nest and fly about, testing their wings. However, they always return to the nest afterwards. Then, in the autumn, they leave for the last time and live alone for two years or so. After this, they find a mate, build a nest and start raising their own eaglets. Eagles are very faithful to their mates and stay with the same mate until they die.

Although marmots may be caught for food by eagles, they do not just sit around waiting to be eaten. They know all about the eagle and the way it swoops down on its prey from a great height. This is why groups of marmots have their sentinels on guard among the rocks, like soldiers. These marmots look out for danger and, as soon as they see it, they whistle to their companions. One whistle from the marmot sentinel is enough to make all of them disappear into their burrows in a flash. The marmots use these burrows to hibernate, which means that they sleep here through the long alpine winter. When the ice melts and the air grows warmer in the spring, they wake up.

Spring is a very busy time for the little marmots. As the saxifrage and yellow flowers of the alpine poppy bloom on the

2

1

The world of the marmots

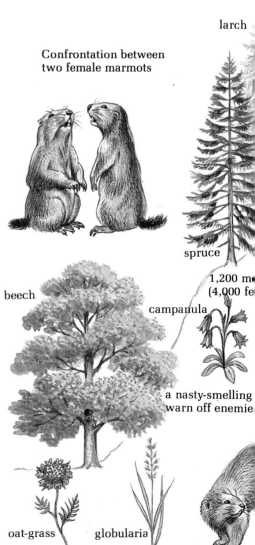

Confrontation between two female marmots

larch

spruce

1,200 m (4,000 fe

beech

campanula

a nasty-smelling warn off enemie

oat-grass   globularia

24

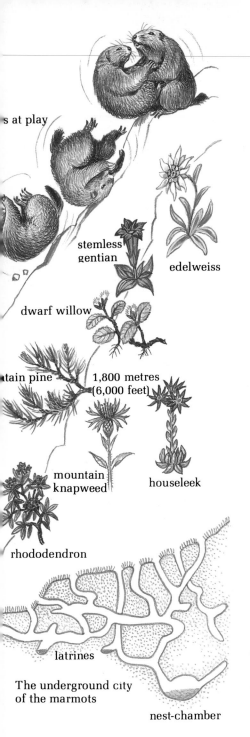

s at play

stemless
gentian

edelweiss

dwarf willow

tain pine

1,800 metres
(6,000 feet)

mountain
knapweed

houseleek

rhododendron

latrines

The underground city
of the marmots

nest-chamber

3

Marmots spend a great deal of their lives underground. They live in a maze of burrows and tunnels which they dig under the high pastures of the Alps. In summer you can often see a marmot standing upright, on sentry duty at the entrance to its burrow (2). These marmot sentries are on the look-out for danger. You will also see groups of marmots playing together (1) or going in search of food (3).

mountain slopes, they are busy clearing up and putting things straight after the long winter. They clean out their burrows and dig out new galleries, or underground pathways. The snow has gone now, so they can tumble playfully down the slopes. If they find a tuber, a thick vegetable stem, they will stand upright, firmly balanced on their hind legs, and hold the tuber in their front paws to chew it. Sometimes, marmots stand upright for friendly wrestling matches with their companions, uttering loud squeals as they fight.

The ermine and the ptarmigan

Not all the creatures who live in the mountains hibernate in winter like the marmots. Instead, when winter comes, some of them move further downhill. Here, they are sheltered in the woodlands when the snow falls and the wind howls. Here, too, they can find food in tree hollows or on the ground.

Other creatures do not move from their homes. Instead, they remain on the snow-covered upper slopes of the mountains to face the wind, the frost and predatory animals who are hungry and looking for prey to eat, like the eagle and the wolf. To protect themselves against these predators, some animals grow white coats: these help them to remain unseen in the white snowy blanket that covers the pastures in winter. The disguise is perfect. If you see a small, white-coated animal running swiftly along the edge of a wood, this is an ermine or a stoat in its winter clothing. In summer, these creatures look quite different: they have brown coats and look rather like weasels.

25

Ptarmigan in
winter and summer
plumage

The alpine
has a straig
yellow bea

The common chough
has a curved red
beak

The alpine swift
nests in cracks
in the rocks

Blackcock confront
each other in the
breeding season

Male hazel grouse
in breeding
plumage

The dipper di
streams in
of insects and

The alpine shrew liv
on insects and other
small invertebrates

Several other creatures, apart from the ermine, grow white coats for the winter. Among them are the alpine hare and the ptarmigan. They grow white coats or feathers when the mountains are covered in snow, and then change to brown or brown mottled coats, with black spots and blotches, when the snow melts in late spring.

The wild cat does not have to bother disguising itself in the winter. This is because it has no natural enemies in the mountains. The wild cat is watchful and clever. It wanders from place to place when there is not much food about, but settles down in one place if there is plenty. The wild cat searches for small voles and shrews and knows the trees which will be occupied by nesting birds in summer. By searching, in tree stumps, it may also find a large, plump insect to finish off its meal.

The common lizard and its young

In the months when the winter frosts and snows cover mountains and woodlands, life is hard and much more dangerous for baby animals than it is for their parents. If a pair of birds were to try to raise a family of young before spring arrives to cover the mountainsides with flowers and swarms of small creatures, the young birds would have nothing to eat and they would die. So, some birds move down from the

Inhabitants of the peaks

ll-creeper pecks
ut of crevices
ocks

The weasel is a
skilful hunter
of rodents . . .

. . . such as the
snow-vole

mountainsides into the valley. Some even migrate or fly away, further south: there, it is warmer, and the baby birds have food to eat and a comfortable nest to live in. The birds will return to the mountains later on, when the young are fully grown. Then, they can look for their own food in the branches of larch trees; or they can hover in the bright blue sky above the rocky mountain pastures and search for food there.

Birds are the only creatures which can migrate over very long distances: this is because birds can fly. Creatures like the common lizard live in a much smaller area. Usually a lizard travels no further than the edge of the nearest wood. It lives among the low myrtle bushes, the small rhododendrons that grow out of the rocks and the short, thin grass which grows between the boulders. Here, the lizard brings up its family. Because of the mountain snows and the cold of winter, the alpine lizards cannot lay their eggs in the earth or among stones where the warm sun will hatch them. Other lizards in

2

3

Like many birds, the male capercailzie (1) is more beautiful in appearance than the female. The capercailzie cock bird shows off his fine feathers to the best advantage during the mating season. At this time, he sings his love song to a crowd of female capercailzies.

Some mountain animals change their colour to suit the various seasons of the year. The ermine (2) is one of them. Another is the alpine hare (3). They grow white coats in winter, to match the snow, and then change back to brown during the summer.

other parts of the world do this, but the common lizard of the Alps must take care of her eggs herself. She does not lay eggs at all, but keeps them inside her body so that the baby lizards hatch out there. Then, when they are properly developed, their mother gives birth to them and they emerge into the world. Soon after being born, baby lizards stand on their tiny feet and look for food among the clods of earth in the mountain pastures. A baby lizard's first meal may be a spider, a grasshopper or a slow-moving little grub.

The black salamander

The black salamander is another creature which is no longer oviparous, that is, egg-laying. Other salamanders put their spawn, or clusters of eggs, into freshwater ponds or lakes. Here the spawn hatches out into tadpoles, and they live in the water for a long time until they develop lungs and can breathe air. Then, the tadpoles come back onto the land to grow into adult salamanders. The black salamanders who live in the Alps cannot do this, though. Unlike the black-and-yellow spotted salamander, which lives in the wooded foothills of the mountains, the black salamander cannot find enough water for its spawn. There are no streams or ponds in the high mountains where the black salamander lives, except when it rains very hard and the salamander's little burrow is flooded. This does not happen very often, so the black salamander, like the common lizard, has become viviparous: this means that it keeps its eggs inside its body until they hatch and develop, and then they are born.

    The salamander is a night creature. At night, the air is

Flowers, butterflies and moths

The argus on polygo flowers

tiger-moth

1

The viviparous common lizard (1) has given up laying eggs as lizards do in warmer parts of the world. This is because life in the mountains is not suitable for the eggs. So, the common lizard of the Alps keeps the eggs inside its body until they hatch. Then, it gives birth to fully developed baby lizards. They are able to run around soon after they are born, and search for their own food. The black salamander does the same.

*   There are many different species of butterflies in the Alps, brightening the high mountain pastures with their lovely colours. The butterflies of the parnassus family have white wings with black, and sometimes red, markings. The lesser parnassus (2) can be found in fresh grass or on the edge of a wood. The veins on the wings of the parnassus are delicately picked out by thin black lines. The caterpillars of the lesser parnassus live on the flowering plants of the poppy family.*

At the edge of the wood

lithobius centipede

beech

alpine rosalia beetle

millepede

alpine salamander

rhododendron

mountain arnica

vitrina snail

Endrosa butterfly

tiger-beetle

reticulated carabid beetle

golden carabid beetle

humid, or damp, enough for the salamander's thin, delicate skin. It is also dark enough for the salamander to remain unseen when it goes out hunting for food. The dampness of night also brings out some of the small animals on which the salamander feeds. These are slugs and slow-moving, juicy snails. Snails have many natural enemies. The larvae, or young, of the firefly are especially fond of them, but the snail's worst enemy is the carabid beetle.

The carabid beetle is a very large insect and a very beautiful one: it is coloured green, gold or blue. Some carabid beetles have a black carapace, or shell, which is covered in decorative round shapes. Carabids cannot fly, but they have six long legs and they can run very fast. As they run, their antennae, or feelers, explore the ground in front of them. The carabids hunt at night, like the black salamanders, and they have no home: during the day they take shelter in a crevice or crack, or under stones.

The snails, of course, fear the carabid beetles. When a carabid approaches, the snails shrink back into their curly shells and blow out a layer of froth to protect themselves. This froth does not save them from attack, though. Many carabids have a long thin beak. They can push this beak into the opening of the snail's shell and so into the body of the snail. The poor snail goes on blowing out its protective froth, but there is no escape: in the end, the carabid beetle eats it. Other carabids eat snails after opening their shells. Rather as if opening a can, the carabids bite off the last whorl, or curl, of the shell with their powerful jaws, and that enables them to reach the body of the snail and devour it.

The tiger-beetle

Unlike the carabid, the tiger-beetle hunts during the daytime. The tiger-beetle is a fine, strong insect, very agile, or quick-moving, and also very beautiful in shape. There is a very eye-catching pattern on its back. The tiger-beetle lives on sunny mountain slopes, and its larvae, or young, dig themselves down just below the surface. The tiger-beetle waits patiently in the sunshine for insects to fly by. Then, its huge mandibles, or claws, catch and hold them while the tiger-beetle eats them. While the tiger-beetle eats, its huge eyes keep watch for the approach of more prey, or perhaps the presence of danger. Sometimes, it will not wait to finish its meal, but will dash across the bare ground that lies between thin tufts of grass. It vanishes from sight. It has spread its wings and flown away, but far too quickly for the human eye to see. A moment later, you can see it again. The tiger-beetle has landed a few yards on up the mountain slope. There it sits, absolutely still, waiting again for its prey.

The wild cat (2) hunts alone in the vast, silent mountain regions. So do the owl (1) and the buzzard (3). Each of these predatory, or hunting, creatures has its special weapons and method of catching food. The wild cat can easily climb trees and raid a bird's nest. It can also dig out moles and shrews from their homes undergound. The owl comes out mainly at night and hunts larger prey. The buzzard, which hunts by day will take both small and larger creatures, and does not mind if it has to make a meal of small insects.

1

The claws of the predator

2

eagle ow

The talons of the eagle owl

3

The claws of the buzzard

A lynz with its prey

High up above, the buzzard soars over the slopes. It, too, is searching for food. The eagle-owl, however, is still asleep in its secret hiding-place: only when night falls does it come out and fly on its great wings down to the bottom of the valley and up again over the grassy slopes. The eagle-owl has wonderful hearing: it can hear tiny sounds, like the squeaking of a mouse, or a bird rustling the leaves in its nest. The eagle-owl can even hear the faint thud of a grasshopper landing on the ground. It can tell exactly where these sounds come from, and can swoop swiftly down and capture any of these small creatures. Soon afterwards, the eagle-owl will swallow them, leaving not a trace behind.

The capercailzie

As dawn breaks on an April morning, a loud, rhythmic call can be heard from the lower branches of a fir-tree. It goes *klik . . . klak . . . klik . . . klak. . . .* At first, it sounds like someone knocking two sticks together. Then the rhythm speeds up, the sound becomes higher and more shrill, and is now like a scythe being sharpened. But there are no sticks and no scythes

1

here: this is the song of the male capercailzie bird. In the lowest branches of the tree, and on the ground nearby, a group of female capercailzies sit, listening. The male capercailzie sings this song every day for quite a long time, and always the females sit listening, fascinated by the beautiful sound.

This is the time when the capercailzies mate and breed, and before long the females are sitting on their eggs, each in her own nest. The capercailzie chicks are very active, and are soon able to follow their mothers among the trees and bushes, where they search for buds, leaves and caterpillars to eat. By this time, the father of the chicks—the male capercailzie who sings so splendidly—has gone back to living alone.

The wolf-pack

Wolves live in packs, hunting and travelling together. Wolves are nomadic, which means they wander about the country-side. Sometimes, the wolves are found in the grim, desolate areas which are too harsh for people to visit. At other times, the wolves are seen on the wooded mountain slopes, or the huge grass-plains swept by snow-storms. All the wolves in a pack understand each other very well. They can co-operate with each other when hunting their quarry, or sharing out the food they have caught, or when they are defending themselves from attack.

Something is always happening on the steep mountain crags or in the valleys or among the swift mountain streams and shady woods. Creatures are born, they are hunted, and they

The life of wolves

the den

Working together in the hunt

The facial expressions of a wolf

fear   ag

32

die. Creatures which were tiny larvae only a few weeks ago are now fully grown adults: the handsome alpine rosalia beetle, for instance, lives in the trunk of a beech tree for the first weeks of its life, then grows into an adult winged insect with long, knotty antennae or feelers and a suit of grey speckled with velvety black.

A single old tree on the wooded slopes or in the valley can contain an enormous amount of life. Insects tunnel through the wood. Parasitic fungi, like mycelia, live on the tree and draw nourishment, or food, from it. Great blankets of moss or lichen grow on the tree. Sometimes, old trees are too weak to support the weight of snow that falls on their branches in winter: they are also weakened by strong blasts of the winter wind. One day, the tree falls to the ground. Thousands of tiny burrowing creatures run all over its bark. More small creatures now make their home in the fallen tree. The larvae dig more tunnels or enlarge old ones. Vipers, weasels and robins come in search of food or shelter. The bark of the tree is breaking down, but moss and lichen still grow on it. Ferns start growing on the trunk. Many years pass, and the tree has vanished. Once, its roots pushed into the soil and it spread branches in the cold sharp, mountain air. But now, it has gone for ever.

2

3

All the wolves in the pack must show their submission to the pack leader

The wolf is a sociable creature and likes the company of other wolves. Living in a wolf-pack means following many rules. Wolves must be disciplined and work together when hunting for food (1). They must obey the leader of the pack (2, 3) and they must collaborate and help each other. The wolf's face can show many different expressions: you can often tell from its face what mood it is in or what it is thinking.

THE WOODLANDS

All is quietness and shadow in the woodland. The ground is covered with fallen leaves, broken twigs and soft patches of moss. Ferns spread their leaves in the moist, cool air and old tree stumps are covered in fungi. Many animals and small creatures live in the woodland, but they are timid and shy. They live hidden away in secret, and they are as elusive, or hard to find, as the song of a bird singing in the distance.

1. squirrel
2. badger
3. edible dormouse
4. coal tit
5. brown bear
6. common viper
7. crossbill
8. crested tit
9. pine-marten
10. willow tit
11. marsh tit
12. polecat
13. red ants' nest
14. beech-marten
15. bullfinch
16. jay
17. red deer
18. nutcracker
19. *Strangalia* beetle
20. common dormouse
21. coluber snake
22. roe deer
23. alpine accentor
24. alpine dormouse
25. stag-beetle
26. garden dormouse
27. *Acanthocinus* beetle
28. printer-beetle
29. wood-wasp
30. larva of wood-wasp

Voices among the trees

As you move along the narrow path that leads to the heart of the wood, the air smells of wet earth and toadstools. Here and there, rays of sunlight find their way through the branches and reach the soil below, which is covered with dead leaves. Here and there, too, you find a patch of grass, or a moss-covered rock or a stump covered with lichen-plants. Small birds, like tits, flutter in the lower branches of the fir-trees. Somewhere far away, you can hear a bird calling. It may be the monotonous *coo-coo* of the cuckoo interrupting the more melodious songs of the crossbill or bullfinch. Cuckoos are lazy and selfish birds. They do not make nests of their own, and have no idea how to build one. Instead, they lay their eggs in the nests of other birds, like robins or shrikes. The robin may leave its nest in search of food, and when it returns, there is another egg there. The robin cannot count, so it does not realise that there is one egg more than its own four or five eggs: and it does not notice that the extra egg is a bit larger than the others. The extra egg can mean disaster for the baby robins. When all the young birds hatch from their eggs, the cuckoo is bigger and greedier than the robins and it is always the first to grab the food brought back to the nest. Before long, the baby cuckoo

2

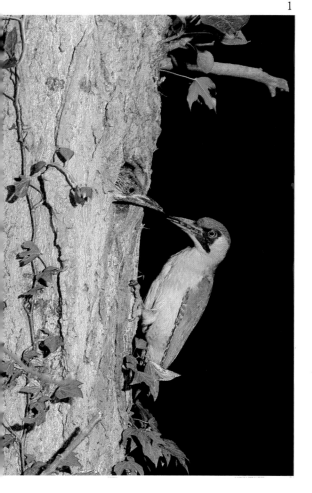

1

Woodland birds

nutcracker

The head of a crossbill

A crossbill plucking a pine-cone

jay

Coal tit with young

An unmistak identifying fe

marsh tit

alpine accentor

A pai of bul at the

willow tit

crested tit

throws the little robins out of the nest. They fall to the ground, where they die. And now, the cuckoo can have all the food and attention from the mother robin, who still does not realise that this last chick is not her own.

The woodpecker

It is not always easy to see a woodpecker, but you can certainly hear it. When it hammers with its beak on a tree trunk, a quick drumming sound echoes through the woods.

Woodpeckers are busy all day, searching for insects to eat. They have long, pointed tongues to lick insects out of tiny crevices in the tree bark. Woodpeckers search for tunnels bored into the wood by fat longhorn beetle grubs: the bird's powerful beak opens up the tunnels to reach the grubs. Woodpeckers work ceaselessly for eight hours, from dawn to midday. Then they rest, and start again, hunting for food in one tree trunk after another, till nightfall. Sometimes, the woodpeckers search for ants on the ground and pick them up with quick pecks of their beaks. A woodpecker can eat a thousand ants in a day.

4

3

Millions of insects live in the woods of Europe. Some of them live underground. Others live in the cracks of tree-bark, even though they are not safe there from the sharp eyes and strong beaks of woodpeckers. In deciduous woods, that is woods in which the trees drop their leaves every autumn, you can find many different woodpeckers. The photograph (1) shows a woodpecker feeding a baby in the nest. The shape of the woodpecker's beak shows that it eats insects: the beak is long and has a small, sharp point. The beak of the European woodpecker is different from that of the North American woodpecker (2).

Another woodland bird is the cuckoo (3). The short monotonous cou-cou cry of this bird can be heard very far away. The female cuckoo is not a good mother. She lays her eggs, one at a time, in the nests of other birds. These other birds look after the baby cuckoo (4) even though it is bigger than the other chicks and often bigger than the adults, too. The picture shows two robins feeding a baby cuckoo.

37

1

The larva of the alpine rosalia beetle in a beech trunk

A Strangalia beetle on an umbelliferous pl

The larva of the Strangalia beetle

Death of a spruce-tree

Ants are very common in woods. At all hours of the day, long columns of ants search twigs, tree stumps and clods of earth: they are like a huge army on the march. Millions of ants live in huge nests that lie beneath great heaps of pine needles. Sometimes, these heaps can reach heights of 50 centimetres (nearly 20 in). Swarms of red ants go back and forth continually. Some bring back food to the nest: it takes dozens to bring back a caterpillar, but ants are used to working together. Other ants leave the nest to take over the work of ants already out in the woods. Others work among the pine needles, enlarging the nest. Some repair the nest's defences or dig new tunnels, chambers and cells where eggs and larvae are stored.

An ants' nest usually contains one queen ant, who spends all her time laying eggs. The queen is surrounded by millions of worker-ants. The workers do not lay eggs of their own, but take care of the queen's eggs and the larvae. After a time, the larvae become pupae (2), and these, in turn become adult ants. Some species of ants look after the aphids (1). Aphids are small green insects which suck the sap from plants. They produce the honeydew which the ants love.

2

Ant trails

Adult ants work very hard indeed: they are always labouring at some task and attending to the needs of the ant colony. Ants start life quite differently, though. They spend their early days as motionless, sausage-shaped creatures: the only thing they can do is swallow the food brought to them by the adult ants. But the larvae grow very quickly and before long, each of them has developed a yellowish, papery cocoon. Inside this cocoon, or wrapping, the larva undergoes a rapid change. Its sausage-shape disappears, and in its place there is an adult ant taking shape: it has six long legs, two antennae and powerful, grasping jaws. As soon as the change from larva to ant is complete, the new ant breaks out of its cocoon. It is very pale in colour and cannot stand or walk very well, but at once the new ant begins to work. Before long, it is crawling up tree trunks,

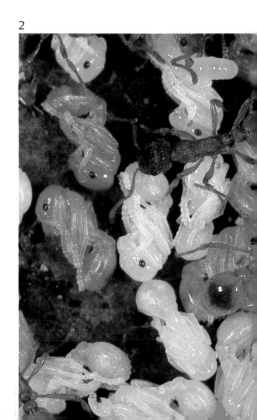

spruce trees

lichens

red ant's nest

following trails laid by other ants who have travelled that way before: the trails are scent-trails, invisible to the eye.

If someone were to wipe a section of the tree bark and so interrupt the trail, it could cause the ants a lot of trouble. Along comes an ant, then another and another and more and more, but because the scent-trail has been broken, they cannot tell where it leads. The ants become confused, and start piling up on top of each other as if they have come up against some obstacle. But some ants are more intelligent than others: one ant will cross the section of bark where the trail has been lost and find the spot where it starts again. The other ants follow and before long, the gap in the trail has been marked with more droplets of scent, and the trail is complete again.

There are a few tree trunks lying on the ground by the path. They were left there some time ago by woodcutters. The branches have been cut off, and the bark has begun to decay and come away from the wood. If you pull a piece right off, you will see a network, or web of long filaments. These filaments, or lines, are white, yellow or reddish in colour. They show that fungi have begun to grow between the bark and the wood. A few small, slimy earthworms can be seen in the thin

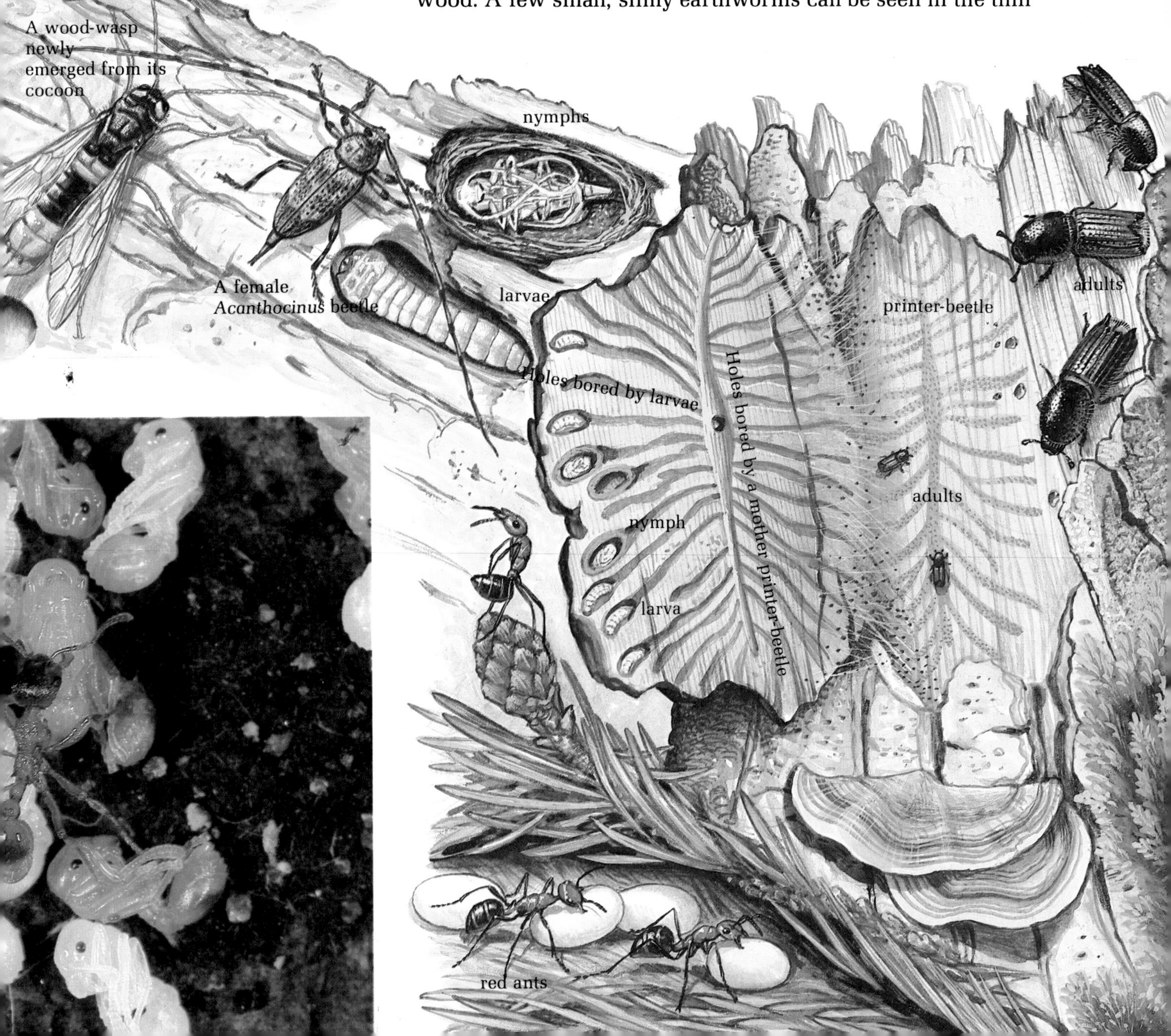

A wood-wasp newly emerged from its cocoon

A female *Acanthocinus* beetle

nymphs

larvae

Holes bored by larvae

Holes bored by a mother printer-beetle

printer-beetle

adults

adults

nymph

larva

adults

red ants

layer of soil and sawdust which is beginning to fill the spaces under the bark: the earthworms move about by first stretching and then shrinking their bodies. Tiny grey and blue spring-tails—minute wingless insects—leap and jump on the wrinkled surface of the tree trunks. They are so tiny, they can hide in the smallest cracks.

The printer-beetle

If you see a large hole in the wood of a tree trunk, you may have found the home of a wood-wasp larva which has now grown up and flown away. It may not have gone very far and could be quite close by. Listen for a loud buzzing noise and look for a wasp-like insect flying around. If it is a wood-wasp, it will have black and yellow stripes and clouded wings. Its body ends in what looks like a long sting, but this is really a tube through which the wood-wasp inserts its eggs into wood. Inside the wood, the eggs will hatch out into larvae, and these will burrow into the tree.

Another insect that tunnels into trees is the printer-beetle. Its Latin name is *Ips typographus*. Although the printer-beetle is rather uninteresting in appearance, it makes beautiful patterns in the tunnels it burrows into the tree bark. This tunnel is the work of a whole family of printer-beetles. The mother starts by boring a long straight tunnel and there she

1

Four seasons in the growth of a red deer's antlers

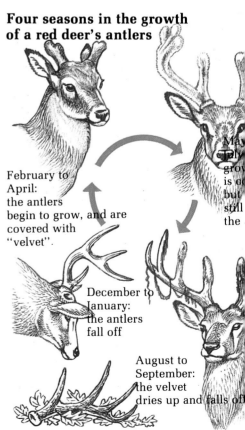

February to April: the antlers begin to grow, and are covered with "velvet".

December to January: the antlers fall off

August to September: the velvet dries up and falls off

40

The male red deer have antlers, which grow longer and heavier as the years pass (1, 2). Female red deer have no antlers. Neither do the young fawns (3) seen here in a white-speckled coat. An old stag (4) lifts his head back, and utters a loud call. This call, which is not very musical, is known as "belling".

2

3

4

lays her eggs. Soon, the larvae hatch out from the eggs. Each larva starts its own tunnel, and as the larva grows fatter, the tunnel grows wider and moves further and further into the wood.

The larvae never collide in the tunnels because the tunnels never cross. Even though they cannot communicate with each other, each larva somehow manages to keep away from the rest, and so none of them comes to harm. The strange thing is, though, that if you look at their tunnels, it does seem as if they *have* been working together. Between them, the mother printer-beetle and her larvae have produced a lovely and pleasing design, which looks just like a fir tree.

The red deer in the forest clearing

It has been very dark under the trees, but now it starts to grow lighter. As you go on through the wood, you can see sunlight breaking through the canopy, or ceiling, of leafy branches. Then the pathway opens out and you come into the wide, sunny space of a clearing in the trees. This is where the red deer lives. The stag, or male deer, is a very impressive beast, with his large body and his huge antlers. The female, or hind, is smaller, and has no horns. You may be able to see the deers' family, long-legged fawns, with white spots on their backs.

41

The fawns are not very steady on their legs. The family of deer will stay together until the winter is over, then, in the spring, the young ones will be big enough to go off on their own. The young males will start to grow their antlers: in the first year, they are straight and are not divided in branches. But as time goes on, the antlers become bigger, heavier and more branched. Deer shed, or drop, their antlers every autumn, and grow a new pair in the spring. During the mating season, the stags fight for possession of the hinds. They fight with their antlers, but the hinds do not seem to care very much: they stand around chewing mouthfuls of grass or bark while the woodland echoes with the sound of clashing horns.

Very often you cannot see the deer at all, because they live deep in the forest, where it is difficult to find them. Brown bears also live deep inside the forest and make their winter dens in the thickest part of the woodland. Usually, these dens are built at the foot of an old tree, among rocks covered with moss. When spring returns, brown bears get restless and start roaming among the trees, following the scent of honey coming from the nests of wild bees. They go down to the stream and catch fish, then return to the forest looking for berries. The bears are still hungry, though, and may pluck up the courage to head for fields and orchards where they can find plants and fruits. Brown bears are very big, but they are afraid of people, especially hunters: because of the hunters, only a few brown bear families still survive today.

Brown bears are up to 1.5 metres (5 ft) high and weigh about 136 kilogrammes (over 21 stones). Animals as big as this need lots of food. They stagger along woodland paths on their hind legs, always looking for anything edible, their huge claws always ready to smash a beehive for its honey or tear bark off a tree trunk.

2

The world of the fox

red fox

The polecat discourages predators by emitting an evil-smelling liquid

A b
at t
ent
its

1

42

A beech-marten robbing a crossbill's nest

e squirrel
:apes
leaping
m branch to branch

A pine-marten chasing a squirrel

3

The viper

Most people seem to be frightened of snakes, even though they have only seen pictures of them. This applies specially to vipers. In fact, vipers, like many snakes and serpents, are very often peaceful and shy and are not very likely to hurt anyone. The viper is not totally harmless, however, though it is much more timid than the grass snakes which you can find along the banks of rivers in Europe. The viper will not start an argument or quarrel, and will not suddenly spring out at a passing human being and bite just for the sake of doing it. The only time a viper will bite a human being is when it is attacked or disturbed.

This might happen if it is forced to leave its quiet refuge in the grass, among the stones or under a fallen tree. The viper prefers to spend the whole day hidden in its lair, and come out after nightfall to hunt for mice and small birds. The viper strikes suddenly and with lightning speed, sinking its poisonous fangs into the flesh of its prey before it can escape. Afterwards, the viper takes its time swallowing its meal. It never strays far from its home.

The woods of Europe are home to many foxes, although they are not often seen in daylight. Foxes prefer to remain in their underground dens until nightfall: this is a better time for the fox to go searching the woodland clearings or the cultivated fields for its food. Foxes will enter villages in search of prey, and like the brown bear, they will eat almost anything.

There are not many brown bears in the woodlands of Europe today. Brown bears are clever animals. They can make their homes in the snow (1), climb trees with skill and swim well (2). They will eat almost anything, from roots and eggs to small animals. Bears are particularly fond of the honey made by wild bees.

43

The dormouse that nests in a tree

Down the hillside at a lower level, you may find a thick beech wood. Here smooth columns of tall trees rise up towards the sky. The red squirrel and the edible dormouse live here. The edible dormouse is a tiny animal which spends a great deal of its time asleep. It is a lively, pretty little thing, with soft ash-grey fur that grows a lighter colour on its sides and is almost white on its belly. The dormouse has bright little eyes, very, very long whiskers and a long thick tail. It is always twirling its tail. You can see that it lives in trees if you look at its tiny feet: they are made for clinging to branches and running along them. The dormouse builds its nest high up the trees, just like a bird. It sleeps during the day, and then leaves the nest at night to look for food. After the end of the pine-cone season, the woods have plenty to offer the dormouse. There are juicy berries, the first hazelnuts, snails, insects and maybe bird's nests, which the dormouse might try to raid for eggs. The dormouse has a very healthy appetite. In September, it feasts for several nights and becomes a very fat little creature. Now it is ready to face the harsh winter.

The dormouse does not wait for the first snowfall before it hibernates for the winter. It begins to hibernate some time in October. As soon as it sees the first signs of winter frost, it disappears into its nest, and curls up inside. Throughout the

1

The sleeping

edible dormouse

dormouse

stag beetle larva

forest dormouse

chrysalis

badger

44

2   3

We always think of the dormouse (1) as a sleepy creature. This is probably because it hibernates, or sleeps, throughout the winter. When spring arrives, it wakes up and goes searching for buds and seeds.

Stag-beetles are very large, impressive-looking insects. Male stag-beetles often have very fierce fights. They use their great jaws (2, 3) to fight each other in the same way that stags use their antlers.

bear

oak

winter its fur coat will keep it warm. It does not wake until the following spring, when the first warm days arrive and the trees start to grow green again. Then, the dormouse will emerge from its nest, yawning. It must go in search of food straight away, though, for the long winter has used up all its fat and it is now very thin.

The journeys of the squirrel

Brown bears also sleep through the winter, but the tree-dwelling squirrel, though related to the dormouse, does not hibernate completely. It stays in its nest when it is very, very cold, but when the wind does not blow so hard and the sun shines, it goes out searching for food in the forest. There is not much food to be found, but the squirrel need not go hungry: it has built up a stock of nuts and pine seeds in the summer and autumn, hiding it carefully by burying it in the ground. The squirrel may bury its store so well, though, that it cannot find it again! Each day in summer, the squirrel makes two long journeys, searching for food—one in the early morning, when the air is still damp after the night, the other in the evening. Sometimes, though, the squirrel stays at home to build its nest. This may take up to four days. However, the squirrel may move instead into an abandoned crow's nest: turning that into a home takes the little squirrel far less time and effort.

45

The badger and the fox

It is a bit unusual for furry animals like squirrels or dormice to make their nests in a tree. Squirrels and dormice are mammals, and nearly all other mammals have their lairs on the ground or under it. Some of the underground lairs are very far down. The badger's lair is known as a 'set', and because badgers are very good at digging, they often live deep underground. The badger is a gentle, but very careful animal. It digs a long dark tunnel, about 10 metres (33 ft) in length. The tunnel leads to the badger's sleeping quarters, where it also spends part of the winter. Like the squirrel, the badger hibernates for only part of the cold season. It dislikes daylight, and waits until the sun goes down before coming out of the set. It emerges cautiously, very much on the alert for danger. If all is well, the badger then starts hunting for fungi, wild raspberries, ants, frogs, slugs and roots. Quite often, a badger will stray onto farmland, market gardens or into vineyards. Although it is a cautious, careful creature, it is very courageous. It will defy a dog who stands in its way when it wants to enter a vegetable garden, and stand up to a fox who may try to take over its set. The badger never attacks first, and in certain circumstances, it does know how to give in gracefully. If the fox is very determined to live in the badger's set, then the badger will eventually allow it to share its underground home.

Foxes will visit small villages at night, often to raid a hen-house, and then return to their homes before dawn next morning. Both the badger and the fox spend their days alone, unless there is a young family to care for. The fox, however, likes to get together with other foxes in the winter. Then, the foxes work together when they go hunting for food or raid villages and farms.

Up to the age o months, the ro fawn has a spotted coat and no antlers

yearling roebuck

The antlers of the roebuck

A three roebuck

1

2

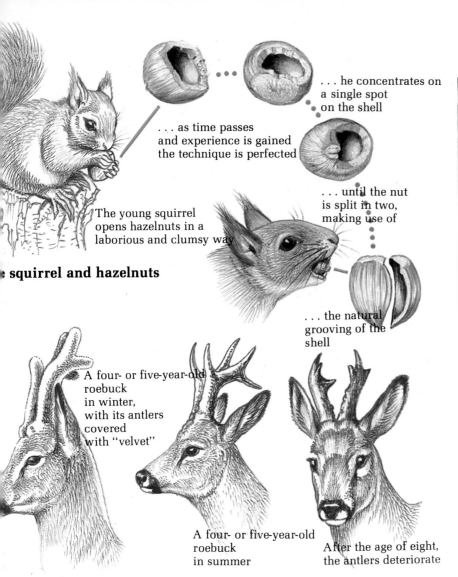

... he concentrates on
a single spot
on the shell

... as time passes
and experience is gained
the technique is perfected

The young squirrel
opens hazelnuts in a
laborious and clumsy way

... until the nut
is split in two,
making use of

squirrel and hazelnuts

... the natural
grooving of the
shell

A four- or five-year-old
roebuck
in winter,
with its antlers
covered
with "velvet"

A four- or five-year-old
roebuck
in summer

After the age of eight,
the antlers deteriorate

3

The millions of creatures who live in the earth

In the woodland, millions of tiny creatures work busily on the thick carpet of dead leaves covering the ground. They break them into tiny pieces, eat and digest them. In this way, the creatures change the leaves into woodland loam, a sort of soil in which things grow well. Fungi and earthworms also have parts to play in creating the loam. The earthworms mix leaves, detritus (waste materials) and soil to make a good compost or manure. Fungi and earthworms are helped by tiny beetle-mites which are shiny and small as pinheads. Little springtails are also at work. The work can be dangerous, though. There may be spiders or big poisonous centipedes prowling among the leaves, looking for food.

The spiders themselves are in danger of being eaten. A sharp-eyed bird may spot them, catch them and carry them off to feed its young. As for the bird, it may be caught and eaten by a fox. The laws of nature may seem very cruel: woodland creatures provide food for other creatures, and the woods are not really safe for any of them.

One of the most graceful and shy of all woodland animals is the roe-deer (1, 2). Roe-deer are so timid that we do not often see them. As with the red deer, only the male roe-deer have antlers. The roebuck, or male roe-deer, has antlers with three prongs each, and they are not very large. Roe-deer live mainly on buds, leaves and shoots.

The red squirrel (3) is one of the liveliest and busiest inhabitants of the woods. It runs up and down tree-trunks like an acrobat. Its long, bushy tail waves about as it leaps from branch to branch. The red squirrel is particularly fond of hazel nuts. It can crack nut shells easily, and has learned how to strip away the outsides of pine-cones to get at the juicy kernels inside. The red squirrel will devour almost anything it finds.

MEADOWS AND PASTURES

Long, long ago, the world was very different from the world we know now. Millions of years in the past, there were no flowering plants, no butterflies, bees or other flying insects. The first flowers did not appear until about one hundred million years ago. The first flying insects appeared on earth shortly afterwards. Ever since then, the pattern has been the same. Every year in the spring, the meadows bloom with new flowers and soon after that, the insects come out and start flying from flower to flower in search of pollen or sweet, sugary nectar.

1. lacewing fly
2. cuckoo-spit insect
3. green locust
4. ladybird
5. aphids
6. mole
7. peacock butterfly
8. lark
9. mole-cricket
10. hooded crow
11. bumble-bee
12. rook
13. swallow
14. swallowtail butterfly
15. lark
16. jackdaw
17. wasp
18. skipper butterfly
19. earthworm
20. barn owl
21. hoopoe
22. blue butterfly
23. ichneumon fly
24. tawny owl
25. cockchafer

1

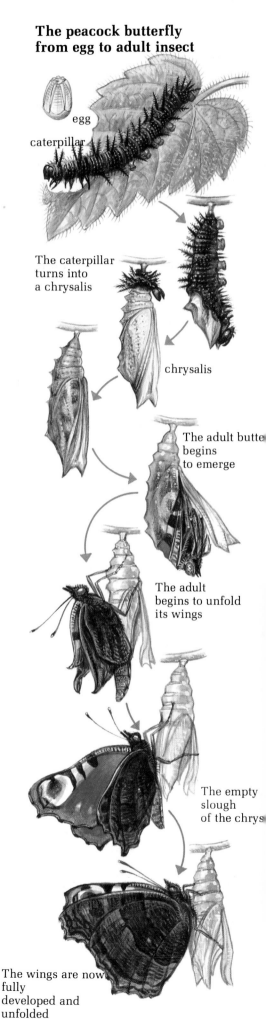

egg

caterpillar

The caterpillar
turns into
a chrysalis

chrysalis

The adult butte
begins
to emerge

The adult
begins to unfold
its wings

The empty
slough
of the chrys

The wings are now
fully
developed and
unfolded

Life on the wing

One of the first creatures to appear in the springtime meadows is the brimstone butterfly, which comes out as soon as the air grows warmer and the first flowers bloom in the fresh green grass. The brimstone butterfly spends the winter months sheltering in a hollow tree-trunk. Shortly before the start of winter, the butterfly came out of its chrysalis, the wrapping in which it developed from a tiny larva. The new butterfly had just enough time to fly around a little on its yellow, pointed wings before entering the tree trunk for the winter. Now that spring has arrived, the brimstone butterfly loses no time in coming out into the fresh, warm air. At this time, it is usually the only butterfly in the meadows. Other butterflies may still be developing in their cocoons. Some of them may still be caterpillars, preparing themselves for the day when they, too, will have wings and become butterflies. Not all butterflies are the same, of course. There are many different species or groups. Each group grows and develops at a different time and a different speed. It is just the same with other insects.

The rose chafers and cockchafer beetles appear in the

middle of March, when the flowers that bloomed earlier in the month have gone: in their place, there are now the first poppies and the campanulas. The rose chafer beetles can be found on the elder-blossom or the wild dog roses which grow at the edge of meadows. The cockchafers like to feast on the leaves of shrubs. They do not stay around for long, though. In three or four weeks, the last of them have disappeared. Before finally departing at the end of April, the cockchafers deposit their eggs in the soil. These eggs will hatch out into fat, white larvae: these have a strange U-shape, and look like sausages on short legs. The cockchafer larvae will stay beneath the soil for three years. During this time, they slowly eat away at the juicy roots of grassland plants. Then the time comes for them to change into sleepy pupae or chrysalises. The pupae sleep for a long time, but once that is over, they change again: this time, into adult cockchafer beetles, with wings, and now they are ready to come out of the soil. When they emerge, they enjoy a short time of feeding and mating among the woodland leaves before laying their eggs in the soil.

The cuckoo-spit

It is almost the start of the summer. The cockchafer beetles have nearly gone from the meadows and hedges. Now little blobs of foam appear all over the grasslands. They look like white froth against the dark green stems of the meadow clary and the yellow-headed sow thistle. Right in the centre of these foam blobs are cuckoo-spits. This insect has been spitting out foam to protect itself from the heat of the sun and from the hordes of hungry ants who pass by. The cuckoo-spit is a very

2

3

Butterflies of the Vanessa group are common in meadows and heathland. One is the peacock butterfly (1) which takes its name from the eye-markings it carries on all four wings. These "eyes" are best seen when the wings are open, but they are just visible on the underside of the folded wings. The continent of Europe has many more swallowtail butterflies (3) than Britain. The swallowtail's yellow and black wings have red and blue markings. Swallowtails take their name from the pair of "tails" on their wings. Other kinds of butterfly seen in meadows include the tiny skipper (2), which is often seen on thistle flowers.

The death of a cabbage white caterpillar

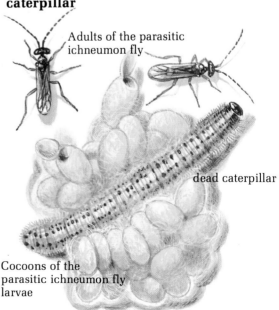

Adults of the parasitic ichneumon fly

dead caterpillar

Cocoons of the parasitic ichneumon fly larvae

1

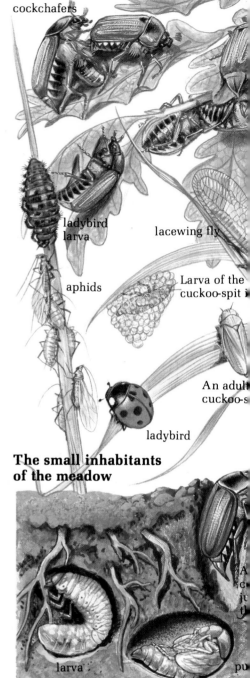

cockchafers

ladybird larva

lacewing fly

aphids

Larva of the cuckoo-spit

An adult cuckoo-s

ladybird

The small inhabitants of the meadow

larva

pu

A c j t t

tiny type of cicada, an insect which chirps very loudly and has transparent wings. The cuckoo-spit does not chirp or sing like a cicada, but like the cicada it does have a short, strong pointed beak which it uses to suck out the sap, or juice, of plants. When partly digested and mixed with air bubbles, this sap becomes like whipped cream. It forms the froth which provides the cuckoo-spit with a foamy nest, and there it lives while it grows. Later on, the cuckoo-spit will develop wings. It does not fly very often, though, and prefers to hop among the plants like a very large flea.

Honey-bees and bumble-bees

Every day, the meadows change in appearance. For a while, they are sprinkled with dots of white, yellow, pink and purple: this is when the ox-eye daisy, wild carrot, thistles and mallow are in bloom. The brimstone butterflies have gone now, and other butterflies have taken their place. The cabbage white butterfly is flitting around, its snowy white wings streaked with black. There are also tiny, brilliantly coloured blues, and lively skipper butterflies whose bodies are covered in tawny red fur. Skippers do not fold their wings when they sit on a flower, as other butterflies do. Different species of butterfly often have their own favourite flowers: they recognise them by their colour or perhaps by their scent. Butterflies always know

Wasps (1) are not as good natured or busy as the bees. They do not make honey or wax, and they are always ready to use their painful sting. Their bright yellow-and-black coats are a warning of danger. In fact, the wasp is warning us. "Leave me alone," it says, "or I shall use my sting!" Wasps are active, hard-working creatures, and they live in organised societies, just as bees do. Wasp nests are made of a papery material. The wasps produce this material themselves from chewed wood and vegetable fibres. Wasp nests are usually well hidden and protected.

the flowers which contain a drop of sugary nectar. The butterfly is equipped with a long, flexible proboscis, or mouth, which they can push into a flower to suck up the nectar. Bees do much the same thing, buzzing around the flowers even more busily than the butterflies, from sunrise to sunset. The bees have to work harder than the butterflies. Each butterfly has only itself to care for and feed. The bees, though, have dozens of hungry mouths to feed, for they must find food for their mothers and also for their younger sisters who are waiting in the cells of the hive.

Related to the honey-bees are the busiest bees of all, the bumble-bees. These have red patches on their rear sections, or all-over white and yellow stripes and are large, black and very hairy. Bumble-bees whizz about from one clover flower to the next. They search every white or red dead-nettle, purple clary flower, or blue viper's bugloss blossom. It is as if they are afraid of missing something important.

The first bumble-bees in the meadows at springtime are the females. At first, they work alone, building cells in which to lay their eggs and going on long journeys in search of food. This goes on day after day until some of the other bees grow big enough to collect nectar and help with the tasks in the hive. But the mother bumble-bee works herself to death. On her last flight to the meadows her wings are so worn and frayed they cannot support her. She falls to the ground, tries to fly again, but she is too weak and dies.

3

The mole-cricket by its nest

earthworm

eggs

brood cells

cells containing honey

bumble bee

cocoons

bumble bee's nest

2

Worker bees spend most of their short lives flying to and fro between their hive and the flowers in the meadow. They gather nectar and pollen which are needed by the bee community.

Other, less busy, insects like the grasshopper which feeds on grass and leaves, live alone. Locusts (3) are a type of grasshopper, but definitely do not live alone. They fly about in huge swarms which can badly damage crops in the fields. Female locusts use a special organ, like a long sword, to lay their eggs towards the end of the summer.

53

Life in the soil

As you will guess from its name, the earthworm spends the whole of its life in the soil under the meadow. It comes up to the surface occasionally, when heavy rain has soaked the earth so that it is like a sponge filled with water. When the soil begins to dry out, the earthworm goes back to its underground home. It leaves behind a worm-cast, a very small heap of fine earth. This earth has been sifted, or separated, by the worm. As the worm moves through the earth, it swallows anything and everything it finds: earth, leaves, sand or pieces of roots. This is not the most nourishing food, but the earthworm has to survive, so it eats it. The worm-cast it leaves behind has gone through its entire digestive system and is the waste in the food it has eaten.

Other animals which burrow in the soil are much more fussy about what they eat. One of them is the mole. Moles have thick, dark grey fur, the colour of lead. Their muzzles are pointed, and they have tiny eyes, so small that it is hard to see them among the fur. Moles have two powerful fore-paws, shaped like shovels, and these makes it easy for them to dig in the earth. The mole is a hunter. It hunts below the surface of the earth, catching earthworms, spiders, larvae and millepedes which have many legs. At night, the mole will sometimes leave its burrow and hunt on the surface: there, it may catch a baby bird or small frog. But the mole always goes back to its dark underground home before the break of dawn.

There is another creature which looks very much like a tiny mole. It, too, has fore-paws shaped like shovels. However, unlike the mole, it has no fur and its belly looks like the belly of a cricket. Like all insects, this creature has six legs. It is a mole-

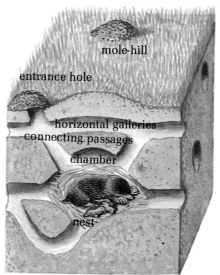

The life of the mole

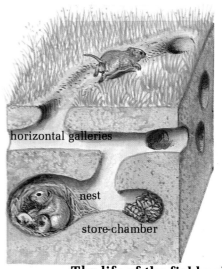

The life of the field-vole

The mole (1) is well suited to its underground life. Its front legs are shaped like powerful shovels, with a wide, flat surface, ending in a set of strong claws. The mole has tiny eyes which are almost invisible beneath its thick fur. Their eyes are like this because they never come up to the surface except when it is dark. In fact they only use their eyes so that they can see where the light is, and so avoid it.

The mole does not need light to give it information about its surroundings. Its pointed nose helps it to move through the soil where it makes its home and where it finds the earthworms, insects and spiders which it eats. Unfortunately, the mole can damage the roots of plants while it is tunnelling through the earth. It does not eat the roots, but looks on them as obstacles which it must dig round. This means that a mole's tunnel can follow a very long, winding route.

1

cricket. Like the mole, it lives underground and is a great digger. The mole-cricket hunts earthworms, and also eats roots and sprouting seeds. Farmers, of course, do not like the mole-cricket, because it can spoil their crops by eating the young seeds.

When night falls over the meadows, the flowers shut up their petals and the clover folds up its leaves as if to keep in the heat it has absorbed, or drawn in, during the day. In the darkness, columns of ants move about. They are as busy as ever, climbing up the stems of plants to reach the aphids, minute insects which sit among the leaves sucking up the sap. But the ants are not going to eat the aphids. Instead, they stroke them until the aphids' tiny twin tails produce a drop of honey-dew which the ants quickly lick up.

By day, a sleepy object to be played with and mocked

The tawny owl by day and by night

. . . at night, it wakes up and hunts

2

3

The barn owl (2) is one of the most graceful of nocturnal predators, that is those animals who hunt for their food at night. Flying almost silently it explores the countryside in search of its prey. Its nest may be in a hollow tree, in the dark bell-chamber of an old tower, or in a ruined building. So, it is very close to the places where people live. If a vole or vole-rat moves in the grass, the barn owl will swoop down and seize it with its powerful, curved talons. The owl's hooked beak then grasps the small animal by the back of the neck (3) and the poor little vole cannot even squeak in protest. The owl flies back to its nest, where a hungry family of owlets will soon eat the prey. The owl hunts alone like this every night.

There is plenty of other life about in the darkness of the night. The vole-rats are around at this time, and high above, the barn-owl is flying through the night air on its silent, downy wings. The barn-owl has been asleep the whole day in the bell-chamber of an old, deserted tower: the bells do not ring there any more, so the barn-owl has slept, undisturbed, by its nest of young chicks. Now, at night, it has gone out in search of food. As it sweeps low over the meadows, it sees a field mouse. Swiftly, the barn-owl swoops down and sinks its hooked talons into the tiny body of the field mouse. The field mouse squeaks in terror and struggles, but the owl has tight hold of it, and flies off across the meadows to its nest.

On warm evenings in early summer, you can see tiny flashing lights in the meadows. These are made by male fire-flies which are sending out signals to their mates. The female fireflies, who cannot fly because they have no wings, wait for them in the grass. The females also have light-producing organs and they use these to signal back to the male flying above them. The male lands close to the female firefly and soon they will mate.

A new day

It is almost dawn. A shiny cover of dew lies over the meadow. Swallows are swooping and darting about in the air above. The swallows are hunting for food. Every time they change direction, they capture a small butterfly or a fruit fly. Meanwhile, the skylark hunts for spiders and crickets on the ground and the crow looks out for slugs and earthworms.

Swallows hawking for small flies

The flight of the lark

The ne of the

A foot a for runn

3

A ladybird climbs up a thin stem of grass, searching for food. It eats a juicy green aphid, a fat little creature swollen with sugary sap. Before it flies off, the ladybird, which is very fond of aphids, will eat many more of them. Ladybirds eat aphids almost as soon as they hatch from their eggs as tiny ladybird larvae with six legs and orange and black markings on their backs. Even at that stage, they look like ladybirds, though they have not yet grown the wings and hard wing-covers of adult ladybirds.

The poor little aphids do not have much defence against the ladybirds. They are sweet-tasting, green-coloured creatures and move very slowly. This makes them easy to catch, and it is not only the ladybirds which are fond of eating them. The golden-eye fly, which has long, green lacy wings, also likes aphids for its meals.

As the sun rises higher in the sky and the air grows warmer, you can hear the busy hum of wasps and bees, the dull, deep droning of the cockchafer beetles, and the faraway call of the jackdaws. Beneath the earth, the busy lives of the earthworms and the moles go on silently and unseen.

2

There are many types of birds in the fields and woods which we do not see very often. Sometimes we do not see them at all, except during the breeding season. The crow, however, is far too noisy and busy to go unnoticed. The crow family includes the rook (1), the jackdaw, the carrion crow (2) and the magpie. The hoopoe (3) is a much shyer bird. It has a sad, mournful cry and a crest that is erectile, which means it stands up.

Daytime in the meadows

crested lark

sparrows
on cultivated land

hooded crow

LAKES AND RIVERS

There are many ways of life for the creatures who live in ponds, rivers or swamps. Pikes, for instance, lead a very calm life. Eels and salmon are adventurous, and migrate long distances. The kingfisher spends a lot of time diving into the water to catch fish. The beaver works ceaselessly. Some creatures can skate on the surface of the water as if it were a sheet of ice. Others live below the surface during the first stages of their lives. Every spring, frogs and toads put their spawn into the ponds so that their young can develop there.

1. grey heron
2. caddis fly
3. pond skater
4. water-scorpion
5. chub
6. flamingo
7. water rail
8. tadpole
9. water boatman
10. pond snail
11. avocet
12. grebe
13. roach
14. bitterling
15. grey heron
16. purple heron
17. grayling
18. gudgeon
19. eel
20. water-vole
21. mallard
22. shad
23. pond-skater
24. water-beetle
25. *Limnephilid* caddis fly
26. blackwinged stilt
27. Montagu's harrier
28. *Salvelinus* char
29. salmon
30. trout
31. lamprey
32. beaver
33. frog
34. perch
35. pike
36. crucian carp
37. *Leuciscus* chub
38. dragon-fly
39. common carp
40. tench
41. grass snake
42. squacco heron
43. bearded tit
44. night heron
45. otter
46. coypu
47. kingfisher
48. bittern

The mountain spring

There is a pool of clear, cool water underneath a large, moss-covered boulder. The water is constantly being renewed by secret, underground channels that come from the upper part of the valley. When you first look into this mountain spring, there do not seem to be any creatures living in it. But try stirring up the bottom of the spring very carefully with a stick. Then pick up a pebble from the water, and you might see the tiny, black flattened form of a planarian on it. The planarian stretches and contracts its body by turns. This is how it moves along. When you picked up the pebble you interrupted its search for tiny prey among the moss stems. Now, you might see two small water-snails which have withdrawn into their thin, transparent shells at the first sign of danger. You may also be able to see a mayfly nymph: it will jump from the pebble in your hand back into the water.

The mayfly nymph spends a long time in the water, while it remains an aquatic larva, that is a larva living in water. One day, though, it will change its skin and become a winged insect, but sadly, it will live for only a few hours.

Around the spring, you can see some smaller, isolated pools in the short grass of the alpine pasture. Sheep often come to the pools to drink. They are not worried by the mass of green algae, a sort of hair-thin seaweed which covers the surface of the water almost completely. At the moment, the water surface is quite still. There is not a breath of wind in the midday sun of midsummer. Then, a skater comes across the water: it has six legs and a long, light body shaped like a cigar. This is a pond-skater and it is looking to see if it can find some small insect which has fallen into the water from the surrounding grass. Perhaps a little cicada tried to jump from one leaf to another, but missed and ended up in the pond. The cicada may try to swim back to the bank on its short legs, but it

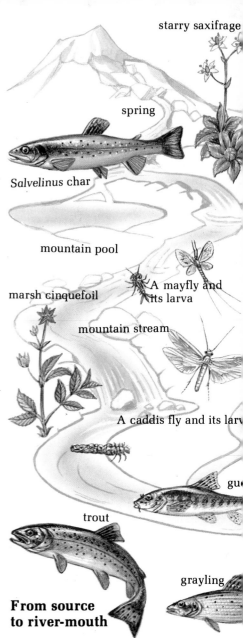

starry saxifrage

spring

Salvelinus char

mountain pool

marsh cinquefoil

A mayfly and its larva

mountain stream

A caddis fly and its larva

trout

gu•

grayling

From source to river-mouth

1

The pike (1) is a greedy and terrifying predator. Its mouth has many sharp, curved teeth and it can eat any of the other freshwater fish in Europe. Pikes can grow to tremendous lengths of up to 1.5 metres (5 feet). The pike can live in waters that are rich with vegetation, or those which do not contain much oxygen, or air. The trout (2), however, prefers the clean, clear waters of swift-flowing streams and rivers. The salmon (3) can also be found in these waters, in the upper reaches of rivers. The salmon work their way upstream from the sea to breed, and here the newborn salmon spend the early part of their lives.

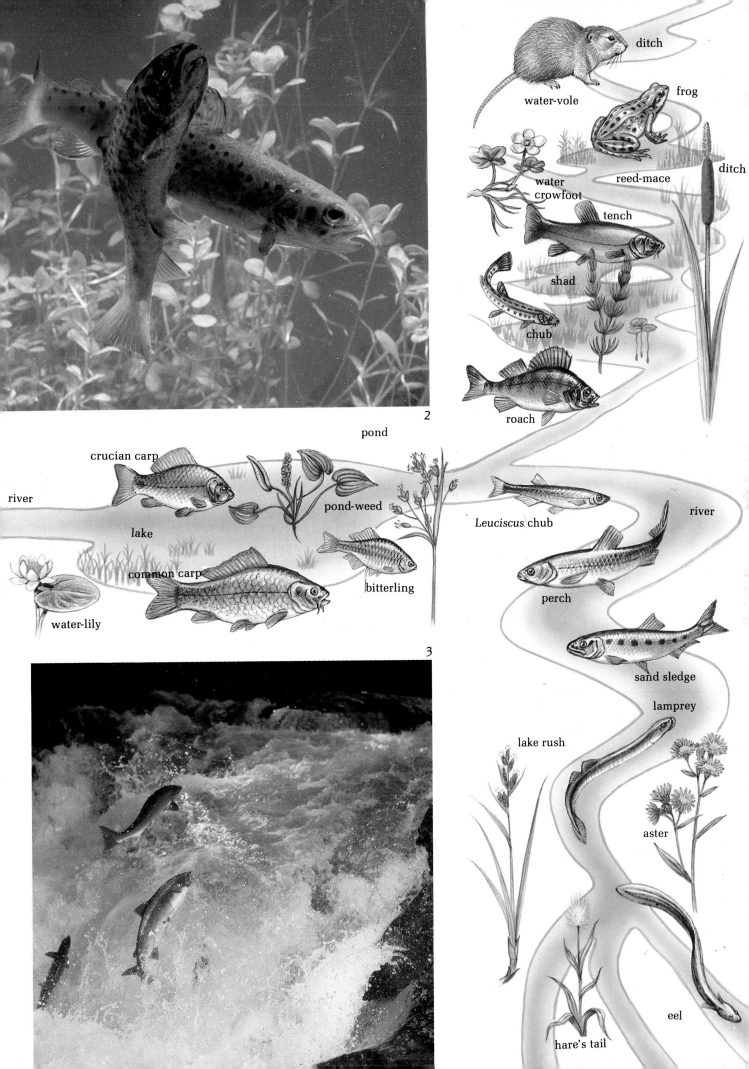

ditch

water-vole

frog

ditch

water crowfoot

reed-mace

tench

shad

chub

roach

2

pond

crucian carp

pond-weed

river

Leuciscus chub

river

lake

perch

common carp

bitterling

water-lily

sand sledge

3

lamprey

lake rush

aster

hare's tail

eel

1

will never reach it. The pond-skater has grabbed it, and uses its powerful beak to suck it dry.

Further down below the surface are some submerged water plants. There are pond-snails among the plants. Pond-snails have honey-coloured shells with a big final whorl on top. Here and there, dragonfly nymphs move quickly through the water. One day, after they leave the pond, they will speed along the edges of the woodland, over the pools and along the streams, searching for their food.

There is a stream flowing out of the mountain spring. Its clear waters follow a route that winds through the grass and stones down towards the valley below. Sometimes, the stream foams as it falls down a series of small waterfalls. In other places, the stream widens out into rocky basins and here, the cold water is deep and very blue. You can find trout here and

Life in a watery world

2

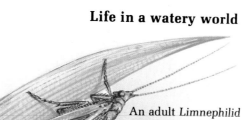

An adult *Limnephilid* caddis fly

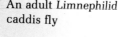

pond-skater

whirligig beetle

lesser pond-skater

whorled water milfoil

The water-beetle renewing its air supply

A water-beetle larva renewing its supply of air . . .

. . . and devours a mayfly larva

The water boatman swims upside down

A water-scorpion has captured a midge larva

The larva of the *Limnephilid* caddis fly

Whirligig beetle larva intent on devouring its prey

opposite-leaved pondweed

A *Phryganeid* caddis fly lar

emergence of the adult dragon-fly

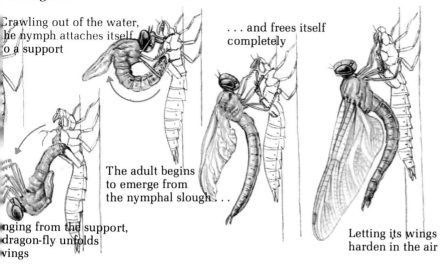

Crawling out of the water, the nymph attaches itself to a support

... and frees itself completely

The adult begins to emerge from the nymphal slough ...

Hanging from the support, the dragon-fly unfolds its wings

Letting its wings harden in the air

also further along the stream, until the stream becomes a slow, muddy river moving towards the sea. Then, you will find the water is full of pike, tench and eels.

The lake

If you follow the river as it moves downstream towards the sea, you will find that the gravel—the sand on the bottom of the river—becomes much finer and smoother. The slope of the river becomes less steep, and the current that moves the river along is slower. Suddenly, the river seems to have come to an end, although it has not yet reached the sea. There are still mountains all around, and the water is not salty, as the sea is. The river has not come to an end, though: it has reached a lake.

There are frogs squatting among the plants on the banks. When they see you approaching they will leap into the water and vanish among the water-plants and the soft mud of the lake-bed. However, the frogs will have to come to the surface again to breathe, so all you have to do is wait very quietly and watch for them. Frogs have lungs, just as people have. Once, when they were tadpoles and nothing but a head with a tail on it, they could live underwater like fish, but those days are over now.

In springtime, when the frogs mate, you can hear a lot of loud croaking on the banks of the lake. After mating, frog-spawn appears in the shallow waters among the reeds. The spawn is made up of blobs of jelly. Each blob is an egg and inside, there is a tiny black speck. Gradually, as time passes, the speck grows and takes a shape, with a mouth, two eyes and a tail. Then, the jelly shrinks away and disappears. In its place, there are busy tadpoles, wagging their long tails like little puppies, and nibbling at the algae or waterplant leaves. After a week or so, their legs start to grow. First come the hind legs, though the tadpoles still use their tails to swim about. Next come the front

3

The water-beetle is a large, powerful predatory insect. It often catches tadpoles, but it also eats other insects, insect larvae, small fish and anything edible that falls into the water.

Dragonflies are also predators, both as larvae in the water and, later, as winged adults flying over the banks of rivers and ponds. The dragonflies return to the water to lay their eggs (2). They mate by the waterside (3) with their bodies bent into strange curves.

63

or fore-legs, and now the tail starts to shrink till, a month later, it is only a small stump. The tadpole is not a tadpole any more. Now it has well developed legs it is a frog and the time has come to leave the pond and explore the dry land.

The young frogs hop off into the damp grass on the bank, searching for worms and slugs. But they are timid and at the first sign of danger, they jump back into the water. One day, like their parents, these frogs will mate and put their spawn into the water to develop into tadpoles and then into the next generation of frogs.

The water has its dangers for frogs, however. There may be a grass snake waiting among the reeds, ready to open its jaws very wide and swallow a frog whole. The jaws of the grass snake are so big that it can swallow very large objects, some of them wider than the snake itself. Frogs may also be in danger from pikes. Pikes move swiftly and silently through the water, and they have strong, sharp teeth. It is very difficult to escape a pike, and these fish are really fierce creatures. Sometimes, pikes will even eat each other.

The bittern

The bittern, a big clumsy bird, makes its home in the thickest part of the reeds that grow by the lake shore. The bittern uses the reeds to make a rough nest on the ground, and it has a reed-like plumage, made of up-and-down stripes. The bittern, which is related to the graceful heron, is a strong, powerful bird and shows much courage when defending itself and its family from attack by birds of prey. Fortunately, these attacks are not too frequent. Usually, the reed bed is

2

1

Many water-birds can be found in the thick reed-beds of ponds, swamps and river banks. Among them are the pochard (1) and the mallard (2): these are two of the most common species of wild duck in Europe.

Life in the salt-marsh

Camargue beaver

black alder

squacco heron

64

peaceful. Here, the bittern stays motionless for hours, its neck stretched straight up. It looks just like a clump of reeds on a windless day.

In the evening, the bittern becomes more active. It hunts through the night, and feasts on frogs and fish. You can always tell when there is a bittern around, because it has a loud, booming cry. When daytime comes again, the bittern returns to the bank to rest and slowly digest all the food it has consumed during the night.

Along the river bank

The river flows through the lake, and leaves it behind to move further down the valley towards the sea. On the river bank, you might see a group of alder trees growing on the slopes nearby. In the water close to the trees, a family of wild ducks is swimming. The ducklings are very young, because it is not long since they hatched from their eggs. In fact, this is one of their first excursions. Their mother watches carefully as the ducklings splash about in the shallow water by the bank. They dig their little beaks among the roots of the water-plants, searching for something to eat.

The ducklings are not the only family living in the reed beds. Moorhens also live there. You can tell the moorhen by its green legs, long toes, strong red yellow-tipped beak, blackish body and short tail. There may be as many as ten moorhens in a family, but you will not have time to count them. They speed over the surface of the water, and vanish among the reeds. There is a mass of interwoven plants among the reeds, and this is the moorhen's nest. The nest is at water level, but it never gets wet or flooded: as the waves come along, the nest bobs

flamingo

marsh reed

bittern

bearded tit

grey heron

e heron

blackwinged stilt

night heron

water-lily

avocet

harrier

water rail

glasswort

up and down on top. The moorhens you saw may have been first fledglings, with mother looking after them. Father is elsewhere, maybe sitting on a second clutch of eggs.

Evening approaches and the air grows damper. Clouds of mosquitoes swarm everywhere. Mosquitoes, like frogs, spend the first part of their lives in the water as larvae: there, they develop their delicate wings and the long, pointed beak which they use to suck blood from other creatures, including people. Not all mosquitoes are blood-suckers, though. The male mosquitoes spend a lot of time flitting about among the treetops, buzzing here and there for hours on end. Then, they go back to sleep among the leaves near the water. It is the female mosquitoes which suck blood, for a very important reason. They take only a small drop, just enough to let their eggs hatch properly. The females lay their eggs in the stagnant water of ponds or in quiet parts of the river, where the plants and silt break the force of the current.

The tiny home of the caddis-fly

Caddis-flies look like small, dull butterflies. Like mosquitoes and frogs, they spend their early days in the water as long, soft worm-shaped larvae, called caddis-worms. The caddis-worms are clever. They build houses made of inner casings of silk, with outer coverings of tiny stones or leaves, or of tiny shells strung together in silken threads. They live inside these tiny homes, which are portable. This means that they can be carried around by their owners.

Usually, caddis-worms can be seen only when moving. When still, they are almost invisible, since their colour matches the gravel, leaves or plant-stems so well. It is easy to see the kingfisher, though. It makes a flash of bright blue as it plunges into the water at lightning speed. It comes up a moment later, with a fish in its mouth and flies off into the gathering dusk.

Night on the river is very quiet, disturbed only by the distant song of a nightingale. The river reaches a coastal lagoon,

1

. . . and c
with a fis

The otter
dives . . .

. . . it twists and
turns under water

2

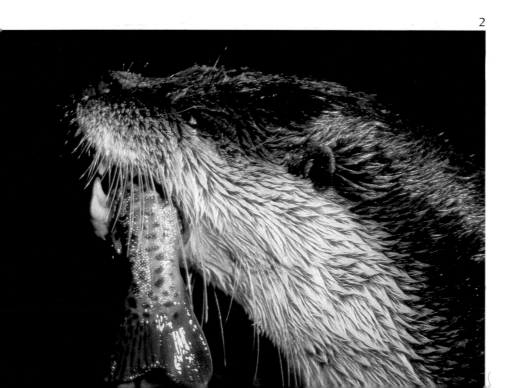

3

The otter needs its thick glossy fur coat because it spends part of its life in the water. Otters are wonderful divers and swimmers, and they can swim easily below the surface and stay underwater for as long as eight minutes without coming up to breathe. When the otter returns to the surface, it may have a wriggling fish in its mouth (2). The kingfisher is another clever diver. It sits on its perch among the branches of a tree by the waterside and waits for the right moment to dive in and catch its prey (4)

where it flows into the sea. Here, the water is brackish, that is part-fresh, like the river, and part-salty, like the sea. The first rays of morning sun appear, and a breeze lightly furrows the surface of the water. Maybe you can see the graceful outline of a heron or of an avocet, a wading bird with a long, upward-curving beak. Elvers, or baby eels, swim along secret waterways as they migrate upstream from the sea into the river. Later, the elvers will grow into large adult eels in the cloudy, muddy water.

You may also see a beautiful flamingo with feathers rosy pink as the dawn. Far away, there is a flock of gulls. This means that beyond the last row of sandbanks, you will find the open sea.

sh have hungry enemies

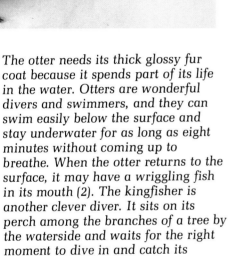

The kingfisher dives

. . . and in a flash it is back on the wing

. . . it seizes its prey

4

DUNES AND SCRUBLAND

The sea is very near, but you cannot hear the sound of waves. Here, in the dunes and scrubland, you will find evergreen oaks with dark green leaves, brilliant yellow broom flowers and pink or white cistus blooms. The blazing sun makes the sand and the boulders too hot to touch. The air is full of the scent of lavender and myrtle. There is not a breath of wind among the leaves of the mastic trees. The only sounds you can hear are the buzz of insects busy among the flowers, the calls of birds and the ceaseless chirruping of millions of invisible cicadas.

1. gull
2. praying mantis
3. eyed lizard
4. stork
5. common crane
6. oyster-catcher
7. Kentish plover
8. Egyptian vulture
9. *Coelopeltis* snake
10. green toad
11. scarab
    dung-beetle
12. collared pratincole
13. spoonbill
14. azure-winged magpie
15. black-bellied
    sandgrouse
16. bee-eater
17. tiger-beetle
18. griffon vulture
19. wild boar
20. hare
21. pheasant
22. great bustard
23. wild rabbit
24. roller
25. fallow deer
26. cicada
27. porcupine

Life in the sand

The scarab beetle is usually to be seen rolling a ball of dung about on the sand with its hind legs. The ball is often bigger and heavier than the beetle itself! This insect has a long and fascinating history. The Ancient Egyptians, who lived by the River Nile about five thousand years ago, looked on the scarab as one of their sacred creatures. The Egyptians thought that the scarab's head, which has a crown, or circlet of short spikes, represented the sun and the sun's rays. From sunrise to sunset, the beetle rolled its ball of dung across the sand. This went on for 29 days and every evening the beetle buried the ball. In the morning, it dug the ball up again. The Egyptians thought that the ball of dung represented the Earth and that on the 30th day, the scarab pushed the ball into the waters of the Nile, where it gave birth to another scarab. This happened every single month.

Of course, not all the scarab beetles in the world lived by the River Nile. But the habit of rolling dung-balls, burying them and then digging them up is very important if the scarab beetle is to survive as a species. Sometimes, the dung-ball is just a

The young emerging from the egg-case

A prayi preparii her egg

Peculiarities of some insects

1

The fierce, predatory praying mantis (1) holds its fore-limbs as if in an attitude of prayer.

Scarab beetles lead strange, but peaceful lives, rolling great balls of dung across the sand all day. This may provide them with food or the ball may serve as a nest for their young. The cicada (3) is another peaceful insect. It sings in the sunshine during its short adult life.

2

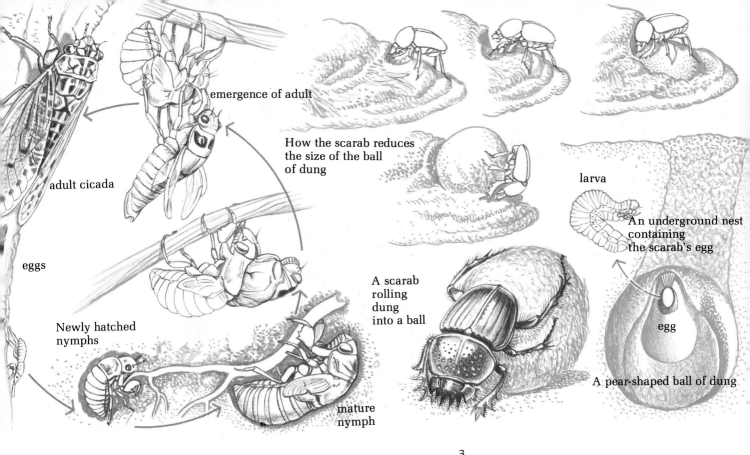

adult cicada

emergence of adult

How the scarab reduces the size of the ball of dung

eggs

Newly hatched nymphs

A scarab rolling dung into a ball

larva

An underground nest containing the scarab's egg

egg

mature nymph

A pear-shaped ball of dung

handy stock of food which the beetle carefully gathers together and wants to keep for itself. In the underground refuge, where the beetle buries it, it will feast off the ball alone. At other times, though, the dung-ball is meant to feed a larva or baby beetle: for this purpose, the scarab beetle rolls a pear-shaped ball and buries it in a safe place with great care. When this is done, the egg is placed inside the dung: later on, a fat, yellow, little grub will hatch out. When the grub has grown into an adult scarab beetle, it will come out onto the surface. There, it will start rolling balls of dung from sunrise to sunset, just as millions of its ancestors have done.

How vultures live

In the sand dunes and tough, thorny scrub, there is always the danger of animal remains lying around rotting in the sun. At least, it would be a danger if the vultures were not there to clear up these remains. Egyptian and griffon vultures live near the sand dunes, and they are nature's garbage collectors. They have very good eyesight, and can see the smallest sign of a meal at a very great distance. Vultures can spot a dead rabbit lying in thin oak-scrub, or a dying snake in a broom thicket, or a weakened wild boar in a tangle of mastic bushes. Once the animals are dead, the vultures move in, but they have to be quick, or the ravens might get there before them, and start pecking at the dead creature. Ravens, however, have only small beaks which are not nearly as strong as the beaks of vultures and other birds of prey.

Vultures are not very attractive birds. They are noisy and quarrelsome, and they may fight with each other as they strip the dead body. But the vultures are very efficient and they do a good job. By nightfall, nothing will be left of the dead creature but a few clean, white bones.

3

71

1

Wild boar take mud baths
to rid themselves of
insect parasites

Wild boar resting
among myrtle bushes; it
has pulled down some
branches to cover
its body

2

Life among the thickets

As its name suggests, the bee-eater likes to eat bees and even
catches them while flying through the air. The bee-eater
perches on the branch of a cork oak, and then swoops down on
a crowd of bees who are busy in the flowering bushes below.
The bee-eater bird is not afraid of bee-stings, and even if it is
stung, it has no effect as it is immune to the stings of bees and
their poison. When the bee-eater catches a bee, it flies back to
its perch with it and bangs it on the branch until it dies and its
sting sticks out harmlessly from its abdomen. Then, the bee-
eater tosses the bee into the air, and catches and swallows it.

A little further inland, among the rich growth of spiny
shrubs and sweet-smelling flowers, herbs and twisted trees,
the rabbit and its many offspring live. The rabbit is a shy, timid
creature and you will not often see it browsing, or feeding,
before nightfall. Once it is dark, the rabbit creeps to the mouth
of its burrow and sniffs the air. If it cannot smell danger and
thinks that all is safe, the rabbit starts hopping around, eating
the grass.

The rabbit is a nocturnal animal, which means that it is
active at night-time. The porcupine is also nocturnal, but it is a

ting at each other's
lers with their tusks

**The private life
of the wild boar**

*The wild boar is the most powerful of
all the animals which live in the
coastal scrub by the Mediterranean
Sea. The spotted coat of the small
piglets gradually changes to the all-
over reddish brown colour of the adult
(1). The wild boar lives on roots,
tubers (stems) and small animals. It
will eat animals that are alive or dead,
(3) and it often uses its long snout to
dig for food in the ground (2).*

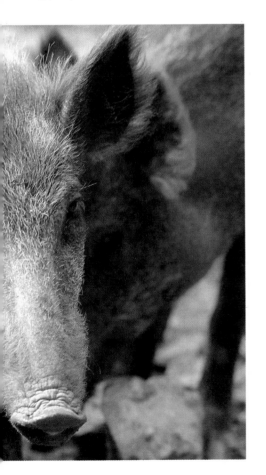

large creature with strong limbs and a great array of sharp
quills. It does not have to fear so many natural enemies as the
rabbit does.

The wild boar

The wild boar does not have many natural enemies, except
man. Once it is fully grown, it can defend itself very well with
its hoofs and powerful tusks. Wild boars live in a large, noisy
group, wandering through the scrub and woodland together,
eating everything they can find. They eat seeds, roots, fish,
frogs, insects and even small snakes. Boars will also dig up the
ground with their snouts, to search for more food. Wild boars
gather a lot of parasites on their skin. To get rid of the parasites, the boars roll about in the mud. This also makes them
cooler. The female boars, the sows, are usually surrounded by
a mass of small, delicate-looking, saucy little piglets: the
piglets have pretty spotted coats, which they lose when they
grow up.

The young of many mammals have these spotted coats; and
the spots are often white ones. Not all the mammals lose their
spots when they grow up, though. For instance, the adult
fallow deer keeps its spotted coat. The fallow deer is not as big
as the red deer, but it has broader antlers. Each antler has a
wide, curved plate surrounded by flat points. The fallow deer
is more friendly and sociable than the red deer, and often lives
in large herds. Herds of deer like to live among the evergreen
oaks and mastic bushes in lightly wooded places.

It is summer, and the ceaseless, deafening noise of the

3

cicada can be heard all around the scrubland. The cicada spends many months underground. There, it sucks the sap of plant-roots, and then it comes out of its larval slough, or skin, and crawls right up to the top of a tree where it dries its transparent wings in the sunlight. Now, the cicada will sing and feast on sap until the sun sinks behind the myrtle-covered hill. The cicada's season of sunshine and song is a short one. Before long, it will disappear, leaving behind a small group of tiny eggs sticking to a twig. In time, these eggs will hatch out into tiny, wingless cicadas with shovel-shaped fore-limbs like those of the mole. Now the cicadas will go underground until it is time to come out to sing their song in the sunny trees.

Dangers in the scrubland

The praying mantis is not nearly as noisy as the cicada: in fact, it makes no sound at all. The mantis has a very long, green body and looks something like a grasshopper. Unlike the grasshopper, however, the praying mantis cannot jump. It has two front legs with sharp edges like saws and these are meant to grasp hold of its prey as effectively as a jack-knife. The saw-edged limbs are folded forward as if the mantis is holding

migrating cranes

A griffon vulture in it with young

Nests on the c

migrating storks

A pair of herring gulls sitting on their eggs

azure-winged magpie

spoonbill

collared pratincole

sandgrouse

black tern

Coelopeltis snake

If a dead animal is lying rotting in the sun, the vultures soon find it. Vultures include the griffon or Egyptian vulture (1). Quickly they strip every scrap of flesh from the bones.

The fallow deer (2) lives in the Mediterranean scrubland. It is related to the red deer, but is smaller in size. Its dappled coat has white markings and its antlers are wide and flat. Like the females of the red deer the female fallow deer (3) have no antlers.

2

Inhabitants of the dunes

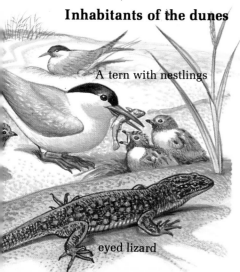

A tern with nestlings

eyed lizard

them up in prayer, and that is how it gets its name. The mantis is a savage creature. It will grab and hold any small insect that comes within reach, and it can be just as merciless with its mate! Very often, the female praying mantis will kill and eat the male while they are mating.

As the sun beats down on the dark green foliage of the scrub by the shores of the Mediterranean, every bush seems to hide a trap for some unwary creature. At the foot of the broom plant, with its abundant yellow blossoms, may be the hiding place of the poisonous coelopeltis snake. If this snake is disturbed during its after-dinner sleep, it wakes up at once. Its head comes up in a flash. It gives out a threatening hiss, which starts very low, but then grows steadily louder. If a sand-coloured lizard hears this frightening sound, it scurries quickly away to the safety of its burrow.

Far away, in the distance, misty haze hangs over the salt marshes which face out to sea. From time to time, you can see a bird rising from the calm, smooth surface of the water. First is the herring gull: it has just finished a good meal of fish. Next comes a small flock of white spoonbills: they have extra-ordinary large beaks which they use to sift, or search about in the mud for food.

A fluttering sound in the evergreen oak tree means that the roller bird has just returned home from hunting. The roller carries a large cicada in its beak. But no one will notice that this cicada has gone. There are millions of others, and it will make no difference that one voice is missing from the deafening chorus of song which the cicadas will sing until night comes.

75

GLOSSARY

Antennae   These are sense- or smelling-organs which are found in the heads of insects and some other invertebrates, or creatures without skeletons. The antennae enable these creatures to detect or discover the presence of scent-giving substances in air or water. These scents are like messages. They can be picked up over very long distances. Sometimes, they tell the insect of the presence of food, sometimes that other members of its species are about. Insects, millepedes and centipedes have one pair of antennae. Crustaceans, like lobsters and crabs, have two pairs.

Beak   Usually, this is the name for the bill of a bird. However, insects can also have beaks. In their case, this is shaped like a tube and it may be rigid, that is stiff, or flexible, which means it can move about easily. Insects use their beaks to suck up liquid food, like the sap of plants. Cicadas are among the insects which have beaks. So are cuckoo-spits and bedbugs.

Beechwood   A woodland consisting mainly of beech trees, with some spruce, ash and other trees. Beechwoods grow in temperate areas, where the temperature is mild and it is not too hot or too cold. There are a few shrubs and many herbaceous, or flowery, shrubs in a beechwood. Beechwoods are usually found in cool, moist areas at medium heights above sea level.

Beetles   A group of insects which have armoured bodies. Beetles have one pair of wings (the elytra) which have been transformed into hard coverings: these cannot be used to fly, but they protect the beetle's other pair of wings. These "flying" wings are formed from membranes, a sheet-like kind of tissue. The elytra also protect the beetle's abdomen, or belly, the softest part of its body. The beetle group includes ladybirds, cockchafers, scarabs, and many others.

Cicada   This insect is best known for the shrill continuous song it utters during the hottest time of the day. It sings this song as it sits among the branches of a tree or shrub, sucking sugary sap. The cicada makes this sound by using its abdomen like a drum: it distorts, or changes, the "drum" by pushing it first one way and then the other, using two powerful groups of muscles.

Cocoon   A covering which protects a caterpillar or other insect larva at the end of its larval, or baby, period. The cocoon is usually made of silk spun by the caterpillar itself. It protects the creature inside while it changes into a motionless chrysalis, and then into a winged adult insect. When the adult no longer needs the cocoon as protection, it breaks out and flies away.

Flowerhead   A group of small flowers or florets which grow together on the same stem. Clover and daisy are among the flowers which form these flower-heads. Each floret is very small. They grow very close together, on the same level, and so they appear to form a single flower or blossom. The white petals of the ox-eye daisy, for instance, are not really petals at all: each one is a separate floret.

Hibernation   A long deep sleep or a period of unconsciousness. Certain animals sleep like this during the European winter. In other parts of the world, some animals sleep in the same way during the hot summer: this is known as "aestivation". When an animal hibernates, its breathing is reduced, its blood does not circulate round its body so quickly, and its body temperature drops.

Hyphae   All fungi, like mushrooms, have hyphae. These are long filaments or strings and they are the basic structure from which the fungi are built. Hyphae may be white, red, yellow, brown or black. Hyphae often form a soft web, like felt, under the bark of old tree-trunks. They can also be found in piles of leaves or on the roots of trees. Masses of hyphae develop from these webs and become the fruit-bodies, often a toadstool complete with stalk, cap and gills.

Larva   Larva (plural larvae) is the name given to the young of many insects and other creatures which come out of the egg looking different from the adults of the same species. Caterpillars, for example, become adult butterflies or moths. Tadpoles become frogs or toads. Naturally, great changes must take place before a larva becomes an adult: the change is known as "metamorphosis". See also "metamorphosis".

Larval slough   This is the empty skin left behind by an insect larva which has grown too big for it. After the larva sheds its old skin, it grows a new one. The whole process is known as "moulting". Adult insects do not moult. This is because they do not grow any more after becoming of adult size.

Mandible   The name scientists give to the jaw, used for the gathering and/or the chewing of food. Insects have a pair of mandibles. The mandibles of grasshoppers, scarab beetles and caterpillars can be quite complicated in shape. These mandibles are used to chew leaves, wood and other tough substances. The name "mandible" is also given to the lower jaw of human beings and other vertebrates (creatures with skeletons).

Matriarchal society These are societies or groups ruled by an old female. Societies of bees and ants are like this. Here, the queen bee or queen ant is the mother of all the other members in the group.

Metamorphosis The great change which takes place over many insects and other creatures at an early stage in their lives, when they pass from the larval to the adult state. In many cases, creatures remain inactive during metamorphosis. Among creatures of this kind are flies, cockchafers and butterflies: their grubs or caterpillars are transformed from larvae to motionless pupae (chrysalises) which are often protected by a cocoon. After this, the creatures finally emerge as winged adult insects. See also *Larva*.

Migration Migration means the regular journeys made each year by many birds and other creatures. They migrate to places where there is plenty of food for them and their young. Many species of birds migrate to warmer parts of the world when winter approaches. They return in the following spring. Sea creatures also migrate. Eels migrate down rivers to breed and produce their families in the sea. Salmon migrate up rivers to breed in the clean, fresh waters of the upper parts of the streams.

Nectar A sugary liquid produced by many plants. Bees love nectar and so do butterflies and many other insects. The nectar is usually placed deep down in the corolla, or the inner envelope, of the flower. While reaching for the nectar, the insect's body rubs on some of the stamens of the flower. In this way, it picks up a small amount of sticky pollen. Later, it will deposit, or leave, this pollen on another flower of the same species. This is how pollination occurs (see *Pollen*), and as a result seeds develop into flowering plants.

Outlet Lakes have outlets. These are channels, streams or rivers which carry water away from the lake. The outlet may lead directly from the lake to the sea, or it may become the tributary of another river. A tributary is a small river flowing into a larger one. If a lake is very far from the sea, it may have no outlet at all. Some lakes have only a short outlet which flows into the dry sand of the desert and sinks into the ground. A river that flows into the top end of a lake, the opposite end to the outlet, is known as a "feeder" river.

Parasite A parasite is an organism or tiny living creature which lives on the body of another creature and gets food from it. This does not mean that the parasite kills its "host", like one creature killing another for food, or a plant-eating creature devouring a plant. There are external (outside) parasites, such as ticks and mosquitoes, which suck blood. There are internal (inside) parasites which develop in the liver or the bloodstream of the host creature. Some parasites live in the host's intestine, and take food which the host has already digested. One of these parasites is the tapeworm.

Pollen Pollen is a powdery, coloured substance produced by the stamens of a flowering plant. This substance is made up of minute little pieces or particles called "pollen grains". Every pollen grain can give rise to a seed, but in order to do so, it has to reach the pistil, or the female part, of another flower of the same species. Pollination is the transfer of grains from one plant to another. Some plants are pollinated by the wind, others by water or by insects like bees.

Sap A liquid which circulates, or goes round, in the body of plants. Sap circulates by means of a network of veins which lead through roots, stem, branches and leaves. It consists mainly of water, but various substances are dissolved in it. Rising sap, which makes its way up from the roots, is rich in mineral salts that come from the soil. Rising sap does not contain much sugar. Falling sap, which makes its way down from the leaves, is rich in sugar produced by the plant with the aid of the sun's rays.

Viviparous A viviparous animal is one which does not lay eggs. Instead, it gives birth to live young. These young are, of course, smaller than the adult, but they can often do things for themselves. For example, they can stand up soon after they are born and search for their own food. Creatures who lay eggs are known as "oviparous". There are also creatures who are "oviviviparous". Vipers and common lizards, for instance, are covered by a thin membrane while they are still inside their mothers. This membrane is a sort of eggshell. In the word oviviviparous "ovi-" stands for "egg" and "vivi-" stands for "living" or "live". Fully viviparous creatures, whose unborn young do not have this membrane covering, develop in a way that makes them much closer to their mothers. To sum up,
"Viviparous": means giving birth to live young
"Oviparous": means giving birth by laying eggs in which the young develop and then hatch out.
"Oviviviparous": is a mixture of the first two. It means that the young develop inside their mother, covered by a membrane which is something like the shell of an egg.

INDEX

Page numbers in italic type indicate illustrations.

Photographic acknowledgements

(a: above/b: below/c: centre)
Ardea, London 24b, (I. R. Beames) 51b, (R. J. C. Blewitt) 55, (J. P. Ferrero) 32, 66–67, 75a, (M. W. Grosnick) 56, (C. R. Knights) 26, (A. Lindau) 27b, 64–65, (J. Mason) 70s, (P. Morris) 54, Bruce Coleman Ltd, London (J. Burton) 45, 51a, 52, 61a, (M. Dakin) 53b, (G. Dorè) 28, (N. Fox-Davies) 10–11, (U. Hirsch) 33a, (J. Markham) 36b, 67a, (Pekka Helo) 30a, (F. Polking) 67b, (H. Reinhard) 30b, 40, 44, 46s, 72, 73, (F. Sauer) 38–39, (K. Taylor) 38, 53a, (R. Thompson—F. W. Lane) 61b, (P. Ward) 50, (R. Wilmshurst) 12–13, 56–57; G. Gerster Zurich 18–19; Robert Harding Picture Library, London 75s, (Photri) 36a; Jacacana, Paris (Casino) 63, (M. Danegger GDT) 6–7, (Ermie) 25, (Labat J. M.) 62a, (A. Rainon) 40–41, (Varin-Visage) 8–9, 37b, (Veiller) 71, (Ziesler) 24a; G. Mazza, Montecarlo 18b, 19a; Nature, Chamalieres (D. S. Berthon-Chaumeton) 14–15, 74, (Chaumeton) 42ad, 60, (Chaumeton-Chantelat) 37a, 57; (Chaumeton-Lanceau) 19b, 29, (Ferrero) 22s, 22–23, (Lamaison) 18a, (Lanceau-Visage) 22bd, 33b, 42bs, 46d, 64, 66, (Samba) 72–73, (Visage) 2, 31; The Natural History Photographic Agency, Saltwood (S. Dalton) 70d, (J. Good) 41a, (W. J. C. Murray) 62b; Oxford Scientific Film Ltd., Oxford (John Paling) 47; Press-tige Pictures Ltd., Norwich (D. Avon & T. Tilford) 27a, 43; Tony Stone Photolibrary Ltd., London 41b.